Praise for Eat the Elephant

"Having known David in business for the past 25 years as both a client and candidate of my recruitment business, I thoroughly recommend David's book *Eat the Elephant* as providing valuable insights into business success and great leadership. David has a strong blend of small and large business knowhow and expertise honed over the past 30 years as a freelance owner, a director of an SME and a senior manager of large businesses."

GEOFF SOUTHBY, AUSTRALIAN RULES FOOTBALL (AFL) LEGEND AND PREMIERSHIP PLAYER

"An entertaining and informative read for any founder, manager or worker with limited business experience. From our experience, new businesses grow rapidly and without an MBA there is a lot to learn in a short time to achieve success. David covers important business topics and concepts in a light hearted and easy to read way, drawing on his own and others' personal experiences."

CARMEL AND KARL SABLJAK, CO-FOUNDERS REALESTATE.COM (REA GROUP LTD)

"David's book is written from his real and broad experiences of living through the trials and tribulations of building a successful business. It will motivate managers and business owners, spark fresh ideas and will inspire them to do things differently. Using his skills and experience and the concepts in this book, David was responsible for a major cultural and commercial turn around in one of our businesses and now sits on our board. This is an easy read that repays the effort ten-fold."

JOHN VALMORBIDA, OWNER JOVAL WINE GROUP

"Spiced with relevant quotes for each chapter and laced with personal anecdotes from his full life, travels and all the successes, trepidations and failures of running his own 'real' company, David weaves a path through everything any aspiring leader would want to know about leading a business to success and keeping it relevant. I love the personal stories and personal learnings we can all benefit from.

Having grown up in Africa myself (and actually eaten elephant) and run my own plus coached so many other businesses, I can vouch for the advice on eating this elephant David shares in this great book. He's truly 'been there and done that'. Don't miss the opportunity to avail yourself of his valuable insights for your success."

HEINER KARST, INTERNATIONAL BUSINESS AND EXECUTIVE COACH

"This book provides great reminders for leaders and managers when they are deep in the challenges of solving business problems. It provides practical assistance using humour and relevant examples to explain management practice. I have used the business foundations advice shared by David with the start-ups I am involved with."

LISA GALBRAITH, ENTREPRENEUR MENTOR AND ANGEL INVESTOR

"A brilliant read that anyone running a business or in a leadership role will glean so much from. As a business owner, leader and working with leaders myself, the content, insights and references to real life stories really resonated with me. David has written this book in such a practical and light way and the anecdotes, quotes and illustrations made it a fun and entertaining read. I loved digesting one bite at a time within each chapter and the flow of the key title and message 'Eat the Elephant' was congruent throughout. The mix of stories, case studies, David's experience and applicable questions to ponder made this book a valuable read and ongoing resource to reference."

RENÉE GIARRUSSO, LEADERSHIP & COMMUNICATION EXPERT, AUTHOR, SPEAKER, TRAINER & COACH

EAT THE ELEPHANT

SOLVE YOUR BUSINESS PROBLEMS IN SMALL BITES

(EVEN WHEN IT SEEMS IMPOSSIBLE)

David L Grieve

5 DIMENSIONZ
PUBLISHING

First published in 2019
Five Dimensionz Press
Copyright © David Grieve 2019
david@5-dimensionz.com.au
The moral rights of the author have been asserted.

Cover design by Jacqui Grieve
(Spurr of the Moment Design – www.sotmdesign.com.au)
Cartoons by Bettina Graham
Illustrations and Diagrams by Laurinda Grieve
Printed by IngramSpark (www.ingramspark.com)
Typeset in Acumin Pro and Caslon 12/17pt by Typography Studio

DISCLAIMER
The material in this publication is of the nature of general comment only and does not represent professional advice. It is not intended to provide specific guidance for any particular circumstances and it should not be relied upon for any decision to take action or not to take action on any matter which it covers. Readers should obtain professional advice where appropriate, before making any such decision. To the maximum extent permitted by law, the author and publisher disclaim all responsibility and liability to any person, arising directly or indirectly from any person taking or not taking action based on the information in this book.

National Library of Australia Cataloguing-in-Publication entry
Creator: Grieve, David, author
Title: Eat the Elephant: Solve your business problems one bite at a time (even if it seems impossible)
ISBN: 978-0-6486857-0-8 (paperback)
eISBN: 978-0-6486857-1-5 (ebook)

CONTENTS

About the Author

David is an expert in business performance and leadership with over three decades working in industries as diverse as steel making, consumer products, education, construction materials and logistics. In 1997 David founded an Australian logistics business for wholesalers. Working with three partners, he created a profitable business and sold it to a global company, based in Hong Kong.

Today, David advises leaders on business strategy and coaches them through leadership challenges. He sits on several boards as an independent director and is a private investor.

David's mission is to improve leadership and management in industry and the community. As an entrepreneur, he has experienced the struggles, challenges and joys of business. He shares the lessons learnt in the pages of this book.

He grew up on a farm near Quirindi in New South Wales, Australia, and learned from his father that the farming business takes hard work, vision and determination. David went to an agricultural boarding school in nearby Tamworth and then onto university in Sydney. He wrote and delivered some of the curriculum for RMIT University's post-graduate logistics program in Asia and Australia. David holds a Bachelor of Commerce degree and a Masters of Logistics.

Married with three grown-up children, David lives in Melbourne, Australia. His interests are his family, reading, current affairs, travel, supporting developing countries, self- education, and sport. David is a member of his local Rotary Club. He continues a life-long passion playing touch football and is a long-standing South Sydney Rugby League Rabbitohs' supporter.

Acknowledgements

My thanks to my wife Vicki for her love, ideas, patience, understanding, support and for editing the blogs. And thank you to my two daughters: Laurinda for using her marketing expertise in creating the diagrams; and Bettina for her artistic flare in creating the elephant cartoons.

I would also like to acknowledge and thank Heiner Karst, Anthony Callinan and Steve Carey for assisting with the proof reading and for their ideas and suggestions. To Kath Walters, my mentor who guided me on the journey of writing this book, for her professionalism, insight and guidance. It was invaluable and rewarding.

To all those who provided the material for the book through both my personal and professional life to date, I am grateful. Also, I acknowledge and thank the great mentors I have been fortunate to have throughout my life. Thank you.

Life is not a destination but a journey, with the good, the bad and the ugly. We can learn from our experiences, and the experiences of others. Wise counsel, listening so that we can understand, observing, educating ourselves, reading widely, and being curious all help us personally and professionally.

—David Grieve, 2019

Dedication

This book is dedicated to my wife Vicki who supported me in this project as she has throughout life.

It is also dedicated to my parents, Bev and Keith. Through their encouragement, support and belief in the importance and necessity of hard work, giving back to the community and the value of education, they have helped me immensely. I remember clearly where I was when, at the age of six, my father said he would sell the farm so my younger brothers and I could go to university. He said, "I won't be giving you money so you have a sports car and live it up at university". Fortunately, my father did not have to sell the farm. However, his intent was clear. In the end, my parents paid for our university education as my mother resumed teaching which provided the vital second income.

Foreword

I congratulate David Grieve on his excellent book and applaud his decision to donate 100% of the profits from the sale of this book to Rotary International's End Polio Now program, which came about through the vision of Past Rotary International President, Clem Renouf (AM) from Australia.

David's book *Eat the Elephant*, shares much with the Rotary End Polio Now program. At the time the program commenced, the goal of eradicating polio in the world seemed insurmountable — like eating an elephant. But we have almost achieved that goal. The number of worldwide polio cases has reduced from 350,000 in 1985 to just 33 in only two countries in 2018. The last pockets of the disease, which occur in strife-torn regions of Pakistan and Afghanistan, are difficult for our immunisation teams to reach. However, Rotary International and our partners, which include The World Health Organisation (WHO), UNICEF and the Bill and Melinda Gates Foundation, are determined to achieve total eradication.

The End Polio Now program is an example of success through vision, having a goal, disciplined planning and sound leadership, which are the same qualities and lessons that David addresses at depth in his book. David knows from personal experience that business is not easy. The process of achieving our goals never stops (either in business or in eradicating polio). When business gets hard, you can go to the pages of this book for some advice about leadership and management, which are important aspects of life. We can all benefit from good advice, so enjoy the wisdom contained in this book.

Sometimes, the day-to-day problems of managing a business can feel overwhelming too. And, although the stakes are usually not life or death, they are high. Health, happiness, relationships, and financial security are all at risk when businesses go wrong.

I thank David for writing this book in the knowledge that it will both be beneficial to businesses and managers and also raise funds for this great program.

—*Ian Riseley*
President 2017/18 Rotary International

Working for a Polio-Free World

Over two billion children immunized against polio, in partnership with WHO, UNICEF, CDC, and other world health leaders.

Rotarians Make a Difference

Rotary International: 32,000 clubs, 1.2 million members, in more than 200 countries and geographical regions

To volunteer in your area or for more information, contact your local club.

www.rotary.org

100% of the profits from the sale of this book will be donated to Rotary International's End Polio Now program

1

INTRODUCTION

'There is only one way to eat an elephant:
a bite at a time.'[1]

Desmond Tutu – Noble Prize laureate, anti-apartheid campaigner

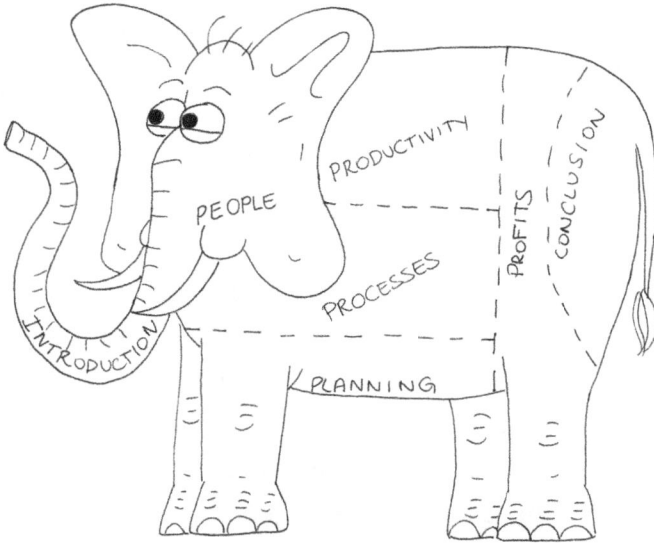

O ver the past seven years, I have been posting monthly blogs on leadership, management and business ownership. The blogs are based on life experiences; my work in various industries; and my experiences as an owner, manager and a founder of a logistics business – and later as a consultant to small-to-medium-sized

---

1   Quote from 2010 US documentary film 'I Am' on Desmond Tutu

enterprises (SMEs). I have been fortunate to have had some exceptional mentors during this period, both personally and professionally. Posting the blogs each month reminded me of the African proverb on how to eat an elephant – 'one bite at a time'. The blogs are small bites and have been revised and compiled into a book. I know they will be useful because both I and my clients have used the strategies outlined in each 'bite' and achieved incredible results. Eating an elephant requires discipline and planning, and so does compiling and posting a monthly management blog. I am passionate about making a positive difference to businesses, particularly as SMEs are the major employer in Australia and drive the economy. This passion extends to the community, whether locally or internationally, and is why all the proceeds are going to The Rotary Foundation PolioPlus project, which I refer to in this book.

Before I go any further, I wish to state that I have never eaten elephant meat. The killing of elephants by poachers primarily for their ivory is a worldwide problem. Increasing human populations and the destruction of habitats are also contributing to the decline in elephant numbers. At the turn of the 19th century, there were over 2.5 million African elephants and about 100,000 Asian elephants. Unfortunately, today there are an estimated 450,000-700,000 African elephants and approximately 35,000-40,000 wild Asian elephants – and these numbers continue to decline. Elephants are intelligent; live in herds led by the oldest and largest female; have long memories; display signs of grief, joy and anger; and love to play. I have seen elephants in the wild in Africa and Asia. As the world's largest land animal, elephants are interesting and admirable creatures. Today, elephants are rarely hunted and killed for their meat.

This African proverb visually describes the challenges of managing and owning a business. How often are we, as managers, confronted with tasks or challenges that seem insurmountable?

The metaphor of eating an elephant describes this dilemma. Being a business owner and manager can often be a lonely experience, with seemingly impossible tasks and unsolvable and overwhelming problems, from people and customers to economic circumstances.

As dedicated managers and business owners, aren't our objectives to:

- thoroughly analyse all situations,
- anticipate all problems prior to their occurrence,
- have answers for these problems, and
- move swiftly to solve these problems when called upon?

This is obviously an unrealistic expectation, as highlighted by the metaphor 'when you are up to your armpits in crocodiles, it's difficult to remind yourself that the initial objective was to drain the swamp'. Although Malcolm Fraser a former Australian prime minister, said, 'Life wasn't meant to be easy', it can be made easier with the 'eating an elephant' mindset. Businesses do have some problems that are difficult to solve, just as parts of an elephant are difficult to eat: the skin, tusks, hair, and feet.

Typically, management books are dry, uninspiring, and easily forgotten. This is an impediment for managers seeking to improve their own performance and that of their organisations. The more successful management and business books have clear and memorable messages that paint a vivid picture. Stephen Covey's book *The Seven Habits of Highly Effective People* is a good example, with habits such as 'begin with the end in mind' and 'sharpen the saw'. People relate better to real-life examples and memorable metaphors which can be used in everyday situations. This book is not prescriptive, with a 'how to' approach with templates to make you a better leader and manager. Instead, it provides some useful anecdotes. They are descriptive and are drawn from years of experience and observation, as well as from nature and history. Each chapter and section can be read separately as 'small bites' on each topic. Having 'been there, done that and lived to tell the tale', I can reflect on what I have done, could have done, or have witnessed, which is useful to others. By using storytelling and visual symbols, my aim is to ensure the message is far more effective and memorable.

I grew up on a farm in northern New South Wales (NSW) in Australia and this proved a great grounding both in life and as a manager and business owner. I was lucky to have parents who were hardworking and resourceful, significant contributors in their local community, and who encouraged and supported their four sons in gaining university educations. Three of us have postgraduate qualifications and own and operate businesses.

One experience stands out from my childhood. I was 12 years old, my parents were away and my grandfather, two of my brothers and I had to muster sheep for shearing. Starting early in the morning, we set out on horseback and mustered three paddocks all at once instead of one at a time. By 3:30 in the afternoon, we had still not finished. The sheep numbers kept growing and became unmanageable. The sheepdogs were not as obedient for us as they were for my father. To add to the drama, we still had not had lunch. You can picture three hungry boys trying to move sheep. This did not need to be the case. Why didn't we just muster one paddock at a time? In other words, we needed to break down the task into something more manageable, especially with our inexperience and having the sheepdogs not cooperating. My retired grandfather was not concerned. He enjoyed proving to be useful. When he owned the farm, he would take all day to muster sheep. This was a management problem. We needed to have the right people, a plan to get the job done, review the processes to make the job manageable and more productive, achieve a satisfactory outcome by getting the sheep to the shearing shed in time, and most importantly, not miss lunch.

That list of what is needed is what I call the five dimensions – or 'Ps' – of a successful business. To repeat, they are people, planning, processes and productivity, leading to more profits. I'd love this to be an outcome. When you deploy the Five Ps, you will rekindle the very feeling that got you into business in the first place: passion. You started with P for passion but, without the other Ps, the passion can get lost.

I used the Five Ps approach in our logistics business. Although there were missed opportunities and we did not do some things well, we were in business for over 15 years. We developed and grew a profitable business, starting with one that was loss-making with less than $1.5 million revenue, and growing it into one which was profitable and had revenues exceeding $19 million – before selling it for over 15 times our initial investment. One of the greatest satisfactions I found in building a business was the personal and professional development of the people you employ and take on the journey.

We have all made poor decisions and providing we learn from them, these experiences are not wasted. Unfortunately, many owners and managers – and this includes me – often spend too much time on activities they enjoy doing or are not important, rather than concentrating on the important activities. While managing and owning a business is often a hard slog and many problems appear to be insurmountable, they can be managed if we are disciplined, focussed, don't allow our egos to cloud our judgement, avoid procrastinating and confront the brutal facts.

How is it possible to tackle what seems impossible? By taking one small step at a time towards a goal – just like eating an elephant, one bite at a time.

Five Ps

Figure 1: The Five Ps

You might be familiar with some of the ideas in the Five Ps. That is great. As author and business philosopher Peter Drucker, who was no fan of management fads, said, 'too often in new management theories the word 'guru' is used because 'charlatan' is too long to fit into a headline.'[2] Some of these ideas will be new to you. Excellent. The aim of this book is to provide managers and business owners with concepts and ideas to help them become great leaders, managers, and successful business owners by providing practical and memorable examples and to make you think and then act. I hope the book is enjoyable to read and useful. In the words of Martin Luther King, Jnr, 'You don't have to see the whole staircase, just take the first step.'[3] You are now on your way.

---

[2]   "Peter Drucker, the man who changed the world", an exclusive interview by David James in *Business Review Weekly*, 15 September 1997

[3]   Manning Marvel and Leith Mullings (Editors), *Let Nobody Turn Us Around: Voices on Resistance, Reform, and Renewal an African American Anthology*, Rowman & Littlefield Publishers, Maryland, 2009 (2nd Edition)

2
PEOPLE

People are the starting point for improving business performance, so people is the first 'P' in the five dimensions of making a business successful.

The initial dilemma in deciding to eat an elephant is that you cannot eat the elephant by yourself. An African elephant weighs around, 5,000 kilograms or five tonnes. If you ate two kilograms per day, it would take you over seven years to consume the elephant by yourself. Then there are the inedible parts of the elephant that must be dealt with, such as the tusks and hide. The elephant also needs to be moved, cooked, and eaten. Even when cooked, the meat will go bad well before the seven years it would take you to eat it.

Clearly a strategy is required to eat the elephant before the meat goes bad. You cannot successfully eat an elephant without asking for help. Leadership is required, the right people are needed for the size of the challenge, and teamwork is essential. Jim Collins, in his book *Good to Great: Why Some Companies Make the Leap and Others Don't* describes the importance of having the right people in the right seats on the bus and getting the wrong people off the bus. That is what this chapter is all about.

There are three species of elephants – African savannah (or bush), African forest and Asian

2.1
Leadership

2.1.1. Are managers different from leaders?

'Management is doing things right;
leadership is doing the right things.'[1]

Peter Drucker – author and business philosopher

Management is the act of exerting influence on individuals and wielding *control* over a business or organisation. Good management achieves this in such a way that a positive outcome is achieved. Bad management has the opposite effect.

Good managers organise, summarise, administer and communicate with other people, departments, and organisations. However, management is not a substitute for leadership. People cannot be managed into responsibility or competence, they can be led there. A competent leader may also be a good manager, but a good manager may lack the inspirational or creative traits to be a 'real leader'.

Leadership is the ability to *influence* the opinions, attitudes and behaviour of others. Note the difference between *control* (management) and *influence* (leadership). An effective manager normally displays leadership qualities. Think of Winston Churchill as the Prime Minister of Great Britain during World War II. He worked in the War Rooms

---

1   Peter Drucker, *The Essential Drucker*, HarperCollins, 2008

beneath Whitehall with the War Cabinet (management – control) while the bombs rained down on London. He also provided inspiration and leadership (leadership – influence) to the British people through his speeches and walking and talking to Londoners during the 'Blitz', providing hope and vision for overcoming the Nazi threat. He was, during this period, both an effective manager and leader.

Here are some of the characteristics of managers and leaders:

Characteristics of Managers and Leaders	
Managers	**Leaders**
• Rely on control of the situation	• Inspire trust in their followers
• Have a short range view	• Have long range perspectives
• Generally accept the status quo	• Usually challenge the status quo
• Administer and maintain the organisation	• Motivate and develop the organisation

Figure 2: Characteristics of Managers and Leaders

Having compared the two, managers can develop leadership qualities over time – given circumstances, training, support and ability. Management thinker and theorist Peter Drucker, in his book *Management*, states that 'the very best leaders are first and foremost effective managers'.

There are six main characteristics of being an effective leader:

1.   Having a clear sense of direction (vision and goal setting)
2.   Communicating the vision to others
3.   Being innovative and searching for opportunities (taking risks)

4. Empowering by building and encouraging strong teams
5. Leading by example, having clear views and being consistent (moral authority)
6. Knowing your own and your followers' strengths and weaknesses.

As leaders – whether at the local sports club, charity, department, organisation or business, we need to develop our leadership skills and understand the main characteristics of being an effective leader.

What do you need to change or develop to be an effective leader?

How can you become more effective as a leader?

2.1.2 A title does not mean you are a leader!

'Being powerful is like being a lady.
If you tell people you are, you aren't.'[2]

Margaret Thatcher – former British Prime Minister

Not everyone in a leadership position is a 'natural' leader.

So, what makes a leader, how do they *act* and how do you *recognise* a leader?

We have all had experiences where we have witnessed or worked for managers who are protected by a title. I can remember working with a person who always let slip in the first two sentences of a conversation that he was the managing director. His sense of self-worth was driven by not who he was, but what he did. While there may be good reasons for mentioning that you are the managing director early in the conversation, most people will probably identify it

---

2   Attributed to Margaret Thatcher though the source and context remains unclear

as a prop and not a sign of 'being in charge'. Interestingly, in this example, he was considered by staff and many customers as 'a bit of a joke' with little or no self-awareness. Props such as your position, background, perceived social position, or using race or gender as excuses can be signals that tell others you are inauthentic and not really in charge.

How often do you go into an organisation and recognise that the real leader in charge is not the one protected by their title?

Whether it is in a meeting or simply walking the floor of a warehouse, it is often quite easy to spot who is really in charge. The clues are normally in how they conduct themselves – whether it is how they walk, their demeanour, their gestures and postures, or just quiet confidence. They appear in control and look the part. On the other extreme, I know a business owner who is often dressed in jeans, scruffy track shoes and a T-shirt. He does not look the part. This is the first step in managing perception. I know he has failed to obtain business through his appearance. Perception can become reality.

Here are some questions that will give you some insights:

1.   *Can we improve our image by managing perceptions?*
   Few people could argue that Margaret Thatcher was not a leader. You may not agree with her politics, however there was no doubt that she was in charge. She never used her gender as a prop, although she was the only female in her first cabinet. Unfortunately, today we often see managers use their title to impress and claim they are in charge, yet you know intuitively that they are poor and ineffective leaders.

2. *Is the use of titles an excuse to tell people who they are or who they think they are, thereby hiding their personal inadequacies?* Maybe they are intellectually dishonest, or living in a fantasy world, or are not authentic leaders?[3]

3. *Who are they reassuring?* Politicians are notorious for using *props* to explain away their failings. They are just excuses for poor performance.

Genuine leaders can manage perception and do not need to use a title as a prop. There is a significant business risk if the person with the managerial title is not seen as the leader in charge[4]. As leaders within an organisation, it is critical that this is recognised. Initially, ask yourself some questions:

Do I look and act the part?

If not, how do I give the perception of being in charge and a leader?

Remember: perceptions can become reality if managed well.

The ball is in your court…

---

3   See Chapter 2: People, section 2.2: Management, part 1: What can Nelson Mandela teach us about being a good manager?

4   See Chapter 2: People, section 2.1: Leadership, part 4: Is Leadership an art?

2.1.3 What is NOT Leadership?

*'By leadership we mean the art of getting someone else
to do something you want done because he wants to do it.'*[5]
    Dwight D. Eisenhower – former US president

We often hear or read about definitions or examples of great leadership.

So, is it important to recognise the opposite of good leadership in either ourselves or others?

John Cleese, the famous comedian, and Antony Jay, one of the authors of the TV show 'Yes Minister', made a fortune from training videos that emphasised what *not to do* as a manager. So maybe this approach works.

A drugs saga in the Australian Football League (AFL) surrounding the Essendon Football Club, which began in 2011 and was still 'unresolved' five years later, provides some good examples of 'how not' to be a leader. In summary, a biochemist began a club-sanctioned supplements program with the aim of improving player and team performance. The team members were injected with unknown substances *with the knowledge* of the coaching staff and club executives. While the drugs may have been illegal, no records were kept, which lead to further unanswered questions about possible long-term health effects on the players.

The club was fined, some board members resigned, and the players were provisionally suspended for the pre-season Cup, pending further hearings. The head coach, the person responsible for the players, went on 'study leave' to Europe for a season while still collecting his substantial salary, taking no responsibility for the supplement-taking regime. The club announced that they would not appeal a Federal

---

5   Remarks to the Annual Conference of the Society for Personnel Administration, 12 May 1954.

Court ruling, stating that to do so would act against the interests of the players. However, the head coach appealed the Federal Court decision, acting in an individual capacity and 'on a matter of principle'.

This brief summary highlights **three clear examples of poor leadership** and, like the John Cleese training films tell us, what not to do as leaders.

1. *You don't take responsibility when something goes wrong.*
   It's OK while things are going well, however when something goes wrong, you start to look for someone or something else to blame. *Leaders take responsibility*, whether it's good or bad. Taking responsibility makes you a leader. That is why people follow you.

2. *You put yourself first and not your team.*
   While the club refused to appeal the Federal Court decision, as they deemed it would 'not act against the interests of the players', the head coach appealed on a 'matter of principle'. This effectively put his interests ahead of the team. It could also be argued that subjecting those for whom you are responsible to unknown drugs is poor leadership.

3. *Complacency or failure to ask questions.*
   The team coach showed complacency or just plain incompetence for allowing an unregulated sports supplements program to be undertaken when he was ultimately responsible. As a leader, you have very *important responsibilities*, one of which is to ask questions to ensure the safety of those in your care.

So as a leader, the people you are leading, whether they are subordinates or people who choose to follow you, expect you to take responsibility, put the team first, actively lead the team, ask the right questions and look after their welfare. Failure to do so is NOT leadership.

2.1.4 Is leadership an art?

'Leadership is an action, not a position.'[6]

Donald McGannon – US television broadcasting pioneer

In 2017, the horrific fire in a high-rise building in Grenfell, London, killed over 80 people. Prime Minister Theresa May took three days to visit the survivors. Her handling of the situation drew a storm of criticism.

Why?

She could not have influenced the management of the crisis. Perhaps her valuable time would be better spent running the country?

However, her actions, or lack of action, depending on your view, raise the **important question of leadership**.

Should Prime Minister May have visited the site and met with the survivors earlier?

The answer is 'YES'.

Gestures are important and her responsibility as the country's leader is to convey to the country her appreciation of the gravity of the event, how the nation feels, and how everyone respects the sorrow of the survivors and those who have lost loved ones.

Leaders are not bureaucrats. Prime Minister May was not the head bureaucrat. A political leader is expected to display leadership in both the good times and times of adversity. **Policy is easy, but leadership is hard**. It requires judgement.

---

6   Attributed to Donald McGannon – US television industry executive

By comparison, one of her predecessors, Sir Winston Churchill, was a leader. During World War II, against what seemed insurmountable odds, he gave strength and purpose to the stand against the evils of Nazi Germany. He painted a picture. This evil had to be destroyed and, despite the odds, Britain survived. Furthermore, this was reinforced by his actions in visiting bombed sites in London, speaking to survivors, and visiting troops as far away as North Africa.

Remember the BP Horizon Deepwater oil spill in 2010 where 11 workers were killed in a horrific explosion? The spill was the worst oil spill in US history – disrupting commerce and peoples' livelihoods, as well as causing massive environmental damage. The CEO of BP, Tony Haywood, stated during the disaster 'We're sorry for the massive disruption it's caused to their lives. There's no one who wants this thing over more than I do, I'd like my life back.'[7] He even participated in a boat race, in a boat he co-owned, while the oil spill continued. Haywood was replaced as CEO within six months of the tragedy. This would seem to be punishment for his appalling lack of judgement and poor leadership.

The former Victorian Chief Police Commissioner, Christine Nixon left the operations centre and went to dinner with friends after she was told of the likelihood of bushfire deaths during the 2009 Black Saturday Bushfires where 173 people died.

She stated, 'Whether or not me being there or not would have made any difference to the fires is a whole other issue.'[8]

This statement, like Tony Hayward's, misses the essence of being a good leader.

---

7   https://www.theguardian.com/business/2010/jul/27/deepwater-horizon-oil-spill-bp-gaffes

8   https://www.news.com.au/national/breaking-news/my-bushfire-meal-changed-the-game-nixon/news-story

A leader understands what is necessary. Churchill was seen to be leading. May's, Hayward's and Nixon's leadership showed through their actions that they did not understand 'what is necessary'.

Leadership is an art and although many gestures politicians make may be insincere, gestures such as being seen at disasters are what is expected. This is no different from leaders at work or in community organisations.

Gestures are important, and communicating your vision [9] to others and having a sense of direction are important leadership characteristics. The wrong gestures can destroy the standing of a leader in the eyes of their team or the public. A good example of a sound gesture is the actions of the New Zealand Prime Minister Jacinda Ardern following the Christchurch massacre in 2019 in being seen publically to support the affected community.

As a leader, do you understand that gestures and to **be seen doing the right thing is a vital trait** of being a successful leader?

A timeless book on leadership that I would recommend is *How to Win Friends and Influence People* by Dale Carnegie. Even though it was written in 1936, it is very relevant today for leaders.

The African forest elephant is smaller than the Asian elephant

2.1.5 Are you an intelligent boss?

'In a high-IQ job pool, soft skills like discipline, drive, and empathy mark those who emerge as outstanding.' [10]

Daniel Goleman – author of *Emotional Intelligence*

It is often assumed that good managers are intelligent, and this is what makes them successful. Is this what really occurs in the world of work? This depends on how intelligence is defined.

Do you consider yourself an *intelligent manager?*

What is IQ?

IQ stands for Intelligence Quotient, a common measurement of human intelligence. The IQ test was originally developed in France by two psychologists, Binet and Simon in the early 1900s, and their work still provides the basis of the tests used today. IQ tests were further developed throughout the 20th century and have been used in many psychological studies as well as in business, education, the military and government.

What is EQ?

EQ stands for Emotional Intelligence and the concept emerged in 1995 with the publishing of a book called *Emotional Intelligence* by Daniel Goleman. It sold over five million copies. Goleman claimed that EQ discounted IQ in determining success.

Why is EQ now considered more important than IQ for success in business today?

Have you met or worked with people who are highly intelligent but have a low EQ? They frequently display a lack of empathy and

---

10 Daniel Goleman, *Emotional Intelligence*, Bloomsbury Publishing, 1996

initiative, are arrogant, refuse to listen to other points of view, are insensitive and argumentative, blame others, never hold themselves accountable and are unable to control their emotions.

I certainly have, and there is nothing more demoralising and frustrating than working for such people. Low EQ people often suffer from **'I' strain** – 'I did this', 'I did that' and 'I am very important just listen to me'. One of the main impediments to achieving better outcomes is allowing egos to override common sense. An important aspect of high EQ is being able to manage your ego[11].

People are considered intelligent if they can reel off facts, retain information or have high technical skills. However, this does not necessarily make them, or the organisation they work for, successful.

While we may, as managers, pride ourselves on our technical skills, industry expertise, and innovation, this does not make us successful managers or leaders. Being the smartest person in the room does not necessarily equate to success[12]. In successfully managing organisations today, we are increasingly dependent on 'soft skills' that build relationships inside and outside the organisation. It is essential to be able to negotiate, collaborate and compromise by listening, communicating, being flexible, and being able to work with others. Management by walking around is a good example of using EQ skills[13]. Poor levels of EQ can make or break customer relationships, create and perpetuate poor work environments and reduce constructive communication with managers, colleagues, peers and subordinates. Michael Gerber, in *The e-Myth Revisited,* identifies technicians as one of the three distinct personalities in business and goes on to say that most technician run businesses fail.

---

11   See Chapter 5: Productivity, section 3: Consistency, part 3: Procrastination and egos cost businesses.

12   See Chapter 3: Planning, section 3: Communication, part 2: Are you a smart manager?

13   See Chapter 5: Productivity, section 2: Change, part 2: Management by walking around

According to Harvard Business Review, EQ is 'the key attribute that distinguishes outstanding performers'[14] and is the leading differentiator between employees whose IQ and technical skills are approximately the same. People with high EQs tend to be happier and have more fulfilling personal lives – as they are more self and socially aware, manage their emotions and tend to be more engaged with other people and events.

The good news is that EQ can be taught. However, it depends on your mental outlook and willingness to change. It can be improved through coaching, training and good mentoring.

Here are three questions that you can ask yourself to gauge your level of EQ:

1. *How would your employees describe your leadership style?*
   Ask this to gauge self-awareness. Does it sound realistic when you answer this question? Do you mention any shortcomings you are trying to address?
2. *Could you do a SWOT analysis[15] on yourself?*
   Would your colleagues or subordinates agree with your self-assessment profile?
3. *Do you know the interests and family circumstances of your work colleagues?*
   This is asked to gauge your level of empathy with others.

---

14 https://www.huffpost.com/entry/iq-versus-eq-emotional-intelligence-in-the-workplace_b_5a56590be4b024fa0543b62d

15 See Chapter 4: Processes, section 1: Essentials, part 5: SWOT analysis

2.1.6 'Do as I say, not as I do'

'For they preach, but do not practice.'
Derived from Matthew 23 in the Bible, when Jesus highlighted the hypocrisy of the Pharisees in the Temple.

What relevance does this have to being a good leader?

Plenty.

Let me give you an example. It was a condition of site entry in our business that all staff had to either sign in or use an in/out who's on-site entry board. Two senior managers rarely did this, despite it being mentioned and noted in safety and management meetings. One day, we had a fire evacuation drill which is mandated by law. This is where the building is evacuated, and the site safety representative calls out the names of those on-site to ensure everybody is out of the building. After the names were called out, you are asked to stand to one side to ensure that the fire safety drill has worked successfully.

In this case, two people were left with their names not called out – the two senior managers. One made some excuses. The other was embarrassed.

How did this look to staff? Well, you can only imagine.

Staff pick up hypocrisy quickly, word spreads and the authority of management and company policies are eroded. Also, the moral authority or status of individual managers is severely weakened. In this case, it seemed to demonstrate to the assembled staff that safety was not important and there were two sets of rules. I witnessed plenty of sniggering and hushed conversations at the time.

These actions *undermined the authority* of management and *reduced the respect for the managers* who did not abide by company rules.

We are often bombarded by media coverage of politicians in safety vests, goggles and hard hats on the campaign trail. While this may seem like overkill, it does send an important message. What would be the effect if the politicians did not wear the prescribed personal protective equipment?

Management is about integrity and leading by example – you can't expect staff to perform or conform to the required standards if you, as a manager, don't. Always do the right thing, and your staff will respect you for it. Don't and you will pay the price, at the least in lost respect and poor compliance and at worst, in an avoidable site injury or fatality.

Doing the right thing costs little.

Are there actions you could do that prove you always do the right thing?

As a manager, *your actions are important* to the organisation, yourself and the staff…

There are three sub-species of Asian elephant – Indian, Sri Lankan and Sumatran

2.2
Management

2.2.1 What can Nelson Mandela teach us about being a good manager?

'It always seems impossible until it's done.'[16]

Nelson Mandela – former South African president and political prisoner

Nelson Mandela, who died in 2013, was an international hero and universally revered around the world as a vital force in the fight for human rights and racial equality. He spent over 25 years in jail but came out of prison not seeking revenge. Instead, he oversaw the relatively peaceful transfer of power in South Africa. As business owners and managers, what can Mandela teach us?

As Nobel Peace Prize recipient and anti-apartheid activist Archbishop Desmond Tutu stated, 'Could you imagine if he had come out of gaol a different man, very angry and baying for the blood of his former oppressors? We would not have made it to first base.'[17]

While I am tempted to list dozens of things Mandela could teach us as managers about leadership, it is always best to keep it simple – so here are my three top picks:

---

16   Attributed to Nelson Mandela, first democratically elected President of South Africa

17   http://some-great-leaders.blogspot.com/2015/03/nelson-mandela-great-leader.html

1. *Integrity*

   Despite often being called a 'living saint' Mandela
   steadfastly refused to be recognised as such. In his books
   and speeches, Mandela went out of his way to point
   out the dangers of deifying him. He admitted to having
   many flaws, making many mistakes and having his
   integrity tested many times.

   In 1985, Mandela was offered a conditional release
   from prison by President Botha if he renounced violence
   and obeyed the law, including the unjust racial laws.
   Mandela did not fall for this very transparent gesture.
   While he desired freedom after decades in prison, he
   did not betray his principles and his long struggle for
   democracy. Mandela replied as follows:

   'What freedom am I being offered while the
   organisation of the people remains banned? What
   freedom am I being offered if I must ask permission
   to live in an urban area? Only free men can negotiate.
   Prisoners cannot enter into contracts.'[18]

   It was almost five more years before he was
   unconditionally released from prison. In the end, history
   showed that Mandela's integrity overcame all obstacles
   when he became the first democratically elected leader
   in South Africa. Integrity was combined with another
   important leadership trait…

2. *Perseverance*

   Despite what many thought was the impossible task
   of achieving democratic rule in South Africa, Mandela
   managed to achieve what seemed impossible.

---

18 Statement by Nelson Mandela read on his behalf by his daughter Zinzi,
    on 10 February 1985

'Perseverance always overcomes resistance.'

How many times in our business life has this occurred? I can remember feeling that a business in which I was a significant shareholder would never sell after two failed attempts over two years. There were times when I was told to 'give up'. However, when least expected, an overseas buyer emerged exceeding our selling expectations.

Opportunities often come when least expected, however, this takes time, energy, focus and perseverance.

3. *Vision*

Mandela had an overriding vision of a multiracial South Africa with a strong focus on the future, not the past. He never lost sight of this vision and did not compromise his goals. While suffering in prison, he was offered numerous inducements to compromise his position and be released early. He declined.

His actions and words left no doubt as to his vision. Leaders with vision have passionate and dedicated followers.

I can remember asking a managing director what his vision was for the company and the reply was, 'For me to be here next year'.

Can you imagine being inspired by such a person?

Integrity, **perseverance** and **vision** are all are leadership traits that Mandela can teach us as successful managers. The outpouring of emotions at his funeral from ordinary people is a testament to these qualities.

As a manager, do you consider these traits as important in per-forming your job?

2.2.2　Are you an ostrich or meerkat manager?

'What makes us human may not be uniquely human after all.'[19]
David Attenborough – naturalist and TV compere

What kind of manager are you? An ostrich or a meerkat?

I have travelled several times to Southern Africa and experienced the amazing African wildlife from a canoe, a 4WD safari vehicle and on foot. African wildlife is best viewed quietly, early in the morning or in the evening. I love watching David Attenborough's nature series. The most recent series I watched was about meerkats. Unfortunately, I have never seen meerkats in the wild. However, I did see some elephants, hippos, lions, wild dogs, jackals, crocodiles, various species of antelopes, buffalos, hyenas, monkeys and ostriches.

This got me thinking about *management styles and the animal kingdom*. On safari, you have plenty of time to think and reflect – watching the sunrise, lying under a tree during the heat of the day or drifting in a canoe. Some animals reminded me of the managers and business owners I have met over the past 30 years.

Think of the ostrich. What do they do?

They run, hide and avoid a problem. An ostrich does not actually bury its head in the sand when confronted by danger. However, they flop to the ground and remain motionless. This passive behaviour only exacerbates the danger and it becomes an easy target for a predator. Not much good if a lion or hyena is hungry and chasing you.

Ostrich managers refuse to recognise reality, do not listen, are often loners, refuse to seek advice, don't act on facts and resist change. They do things the same way they have always done and fail to adapt.

19　Attributed to David Attenborough, British Naturalist and TV compere

On the opposite side of the African animal kingdom are meerkats.

Meerkats are a species of mongoose. They live in colonies of up 40 animals in the desert or semi-arid areas of Southern Africa. What are the traits of a meerkat?

A meerkat sits up, scans the horizon to watch for danger, is constantly alert, addresses the risks and adapts. Meerkats also display altruistic behaviour, watch out for others in the colony and work as a team. This includes lactating to feed others' babies. They nurture, mentor and teach young meerkats to hunt. For example, adults pull the tail off scorpions, a favourite food, so young ones can safely learn to hunt.

Meerkat managers **build strong cohesive teams, are always looking out for others in their team, mentor staff members, look out and adjust for risk, collaborate with others and continue professional education**.

Here are some questions you may wish to ask yourself…

Are you an ostrich manager or a meerkat manager?

What are you DOING to become a meerkat manager?

What should you STOP DOING to become a meerkat manager?

2.2.3 What is a processionary caterpillar manager?

'What matters in learning is not to be taught,
but to wake up.'[20]

Jean-Henri Fabre – father of modern entomology

In the 19th century, Jean-Henri Fabre, the famous French naturalist, conducted an experiment with pine processionary caterpillars. He arranged the caterpillars in a continuous loop around the rim of a

---

20   Attributed to Jean-Henri Fabre, considered to be the father of modern entomology

flower pot, where each caterpillar's head touched the end of the caterpillar in front of it so that the procession formed a full circle. He then placed the favourite food of the caterpillars in the middle of the circle of caterpillars.

What happened?

The caterpillars went around in circles, blindly following the caterpillar in front. Despite the food being less than three centimetres away, all died of hunger and exhaustion. All they needed to survive was to change direction to get the food.

The caterpillars were following instinct – habit – custom – tradition – experience – precedent – opinions – 'standard practice' – or whatever you may choose to call it…

What are the lessons for managers?

1. **Activity is not accomplishment.** How often are you busy but not accomplishing anything?
2. Are you **'caught in a rut'** by following traditional routines, habit patterns or schedules, and not achieving the outcomes the organisation requires to be successful in the future?
3. As managers, balancing tradition and implementing new strategies is difficult. **Success is based on the willingness to plan, fail, learn and move forward**, so the existing strategies support a successful and productive future.

So, are you or your staff acting as processionary caterpillars and mistaking activity for outcomes?

If so, what new ideas and activities are required to ensure continued success?

What habits and activities do you need to stop doing?

2.2.4 As managers, what can we learn from the downfall of Robert Mugabe?

'Only God who appointed me will remove me.'[21]
Robert Mugabe – former president of Zimbabwe

Ironically, in 2017 it was not God who removed despotic dictator Mugabe but his own army.

What are the management lessons from this former dictator's downfall?

Dictators, even when putting their humanitarian and moral crimes aside, are usually poor managers. Most dictators run their countries in such a way that if they were companies, they would have failed long ago. Despite the lessons of history, it does not stop many managers today from doing their best to emulate the world's worst management techniques. Most of us have worked for such people during our working life.

Mugabe is a great example. In 37 years of corrupt, bloody, incompetent and chaotic rule, Mugabe managed to reduce the size of the economy to a third of its size when he came to power in 1980, turning the country from a net food exporter to a country where three quarters of the population now rely on food aid to survive.

Successfully leading a team isn't easy, but it takes a special skill to lead as incompetently as Mugabe. Without trivialising the effects of brutal regimes on citizens, where many 'national shareholders' pay with their lives, there are some undesirable management characteristics managers and leaders frequently exhibit that are displayed by dictators.

What four lessons can we learn from Mugabe's leadership?

---

21   President Robert Mugabe of Zimbabwe in a speech in Bulawayo, June 2008

1. *Inauthentic leadership is not sustainable.*

    While it might appear that 37 years in power implies
    sustainable leadership, Mugabe's leadership was only
    sustained by military force, violence and vote rigging.
    Even his own political party, ZANU–PF, turned on
    him very quickly – indicating that his leadership was
    inauthentic. Without military support, his leadership
    ceased to exist. His departure brought the population
    out to dance in the streets.

    I can remember working for a general manager who
    people did not trust. He always managed upwards and
    ignored his subordinates and peers. When he eventually
    headed the company, there was a rush of senior managers
    to the exit. The business struggled and was taken over
    two years later.

2. *Surround yourself by people who are not afraid to say 'yes'.*

    Mugabe ensured that any potential leadership rivals and
    political rivals were silenced, often in suspicious vehicle
    accidents and mysterious house fires. He surrounded
    himself with sycophants who would play to his ego
    and enrich themselves through his corrupt patronage.
    Trying to promote his wife to vice president and firing
    the in-office vice president was probably the last straw.
    Ironically the 'fired' vice president has since replaced
    Mugabe as president.

    The downfall of many great organisations can
    be traced to the hubris and arrogance of its leaders.
    Mugabe fits this picture. Having a fixed mindset, he
    closed himself off from feedback and saw himself as the

smartest person in the room[22] and was unwilling to listen to others while surrounding himself with sycophants who praised him as a 'revolutionary hero'.

3. *Surrounding yourself with 'yes' people may make life easier in the short-term, however it does not create long-term sustainable outcomes, whether in business or politics.*

   I once witnessed a senior manager surrounding himself with 'yes men' who were sycophantic to his requirements, while he failed to develop them as professional managers. It was a smokescreen so that he could corruptly enrich himself through the business. Like most dictators, he kept his team weak and did not plan for succession. His corrupt activities were eventually found out, he was dismissed and he left his operating division in a perilously unprofitable state.

4. *Blame others to divert attention from your own failings while never admitting that you make mistakes.*

   Mugabe was a master at this strategy. Whether it was blaming the British government for his own incompetent economic management, the white commercial farmers for not wanting to support his government or his political opposition for civil unrest, he always diverted the blame.

On a visit to Zimbabwe several years ago, a local friend, who was not born when Mugabe came to power, privately expressed cynicism about the government:

'Why does the government blame the previous rulers when they have been in power for over 35 years? The Vietnamese are not still blaming the Americans for the war, they have just got on with it.'

---

22   See Chapter 3: Planning, section 3: Communication, part 2: Are you a smart manager?

We see this behaviour in many managers today. They blame the market, their employees, the government or even their customers for their own management failings. We have all worked for managers who have displayed this characteristic. Instead of being accountable for the performance of the organisation, they blame external factors and ignore the cause of the problems. For example, a good employee who leaves under a dictatorial manager is never given an exit interview and their performance or contribution is normally denigrated.

As a boss, are you displaying dictatorial management behaviour?
In recognising dictatorial management behavioural traits such as those displayed by Mugabe, it allows us to ensure firstly that we do not act in this manner and secondly to act if we see it in others. This is the role of a good leader.

What do good team leaders do?
1. Display authentic leadership because it is sustainable and best for the team. They hold themselves accountable for both successes and failures.
2. Surround themselves with competent people, often brighter than themselves and are inclusive of all team members.
3. Develop a succession plan and focus on the issues that drive the business.

Postnote: Mugabe died in September 2019 less than two years after losing power. His funeral in the National Sports Stadium in Harare was less than half full.

2.2.5 'Denial is not a river in Egypt'

'Denial is a very human trait. Sometimes we'd rather not know. We like our delusions. Our favourite bird is the ostrich, head firmly in the sand. Denial may be comfortable, but it's rarely smart (and it isn't a river in Egypt).'[23]

Michel Hogan – Independent Brand Counsel

The above quote caught my attention and made me reflect on why too many businesses fail and why they should not. As managers and business owners, it is very comfortable and even reassuring to deny that the current circumstances are the result of our actions or inaction, and to place the blame elsewhere. This is not leadership but an abdication of our duties.

My business is about working with owners and managers to improve the profitability and performance of their business. As a result, I have come across a large cross-section of business owners, from the really 'switched on' who want and seek outside advice and assistance, to those that are in total denial of their current situation. Several years ago, I met a business owner who, after discussing his situation with me, advised me that 'everything was under control' and no assistance was required. I was not able to really delve into the issues and I left the meeting thinking I was missing something.

After some self-analysis, I concluded that I did not manage the meeting well and ask the right questions[24], which was a failure on my part. Less than a year later, the business went into administration with the loss of dozens of jobs. I subsequently found out that, at the

---

23   Michel Hogan, *'Denial is not a river in Egypt'*, Smartcompany.com.au,
      1 October 2012
24   See Chapter 4: Processes, section 1: Essentials, part 4: Questions and answers

time of my visit, the business was losing millions of dollars per year. In other words, the owner was in a state of denial and, ultimately, he lost his business.

I do not know whether it was **pride, ego** or **ineffectiveness** that made this business owner not recognise the problems. It was probably easier to blame the economic conditions or customers than to look at himself and say, 'Am I the problem?'

Perhaps, it was because the owner could not see the problem even though it was obvious[25]. Unfortunately, we have all seen businesses fail because management is in a state of denial and does not take the necessary action. There are some excellent examples of how denial effects business performance in Richard Tredlow's *Denial: Why Business Leaders Fail to Look at Facts in the Face – and What to Do About It.*

As business owners and managers, we have **responsibilities** – not only to ourselves, but to our employees and customers. A very important part of these responsibilities includes ensuring we are fulfilling our roles to the best of our ability. This includes self-analysis, removing emotions, determining where there are problems and opportunities, and seeking ways to grow and improve.

Remember: **egos destroy** businesses and careers.

There is kudos in recognising there is a problem.

Look at the **facts,** be open to **new ideas, seek advice**, get out of your comfort zone and leave denial behind...

---

25   See Chapter 4: Processes, section 1: Essentials, part 1: Problems

2.2.6 Who's managing the meeting?

*'Meetings are indispensable when you don't want
to do anything.'*[26]

John Kenneth Galbraith – Canadian writer and economist

The quotation by Galbraith sums up what many of us experience
with meetings. Are meetings of value and do they contribute to
improving the operation of a business?

Value is often an intangible concept. The best place to start when
deciding whether to hold a meeting is to calculate the cost of holding a meeting. Using a 'back of an envelope' style calculation, add up
the costs of salaries and their on-costs in time spent at the meeting,
preparing for the meeting and following up post-meeting – as well as
travel to and from the meeting and other costs, including meals and
accommodation. The cost can be frightening.

Once calculated, determine the benefit of the meeting. For
example, if the meeting cost $2,000, did the benefit to the business
exceed this amount and warrant holding the meeting? This can give
you a benchmark on whether the meeting is worth holding. Never
hold a meeting which does not have an agenda that will lead to a
clear outcome. **The purpose of the meeting must be clear.**

I was consulting to a business which held a weekly meeting by
telephone, attended by state managers and operations supervisors.
The agenda never changed. Literally dozens of key performance
indicators (KPIs) were tabled by branch, the managers were often
late calling in and took calls on their phones, the meeting chair rarely
kept to the agenda, and the length of the meeting varied from 30 to 60
minutes. Action points were rarely completed on time. Furthermore,

---

26   Attributed to John Kenneth Galbraith, Canadian economist and author

the business was in financial trouble. Clearly, these meetings were symptoms of what was wrong with the business.

What are the lessons to be learnt from this example?
1. Tailor the meeting agenda to achieve the desired outcome.
2. Clearly communicate the aim of the meeting.
3. Set strict starting times and allocate minimal meeting time for the agenda.
4. Only invite the right people to the meeting.
5. Turn mobile phones off.

Meetings can take up to **40% of a manager's working time** – and much of this time is lost in idle banter, people being late, and people using meetings to delay decisions and offload their responsibilities. Meetings are a necessary evil in an organisation, however the number of meetings held and the way they are conducted must be *managed with discipline*. Otherwise, money is wasted, staff become demotivated, people are not held accountable and little is achieved to meet the organisation's overall goals. For example, one of my partners in our former business – who was responsible for an operation that was performing poorly – would claim in the management meeting that he would implement a plan of action to rectify performance by a set date. Each month we were given the same story and, unsurprisingly, the performance never improved. This not only affected our profitability but also demotivated others and sent a poor message about accountability.

Most people are motivated when they see things being achieved. Meetings can do this, providing there are strict disciplines imposed on behaviour, procedures and actions while also holding people to account. Performance and outcomes must be measured. *Some of the most effective meetings are short stand up 15-minute meetings,* where information is disseminated, issues discussed, and time-bounded action points with assigned responsibilities are included.

There are **three golden rules** for conducting a successive and constructive meeting:

1. The chair should conduct the meeting in a disciplined and professional manner, keep on track and have a clear aim or desired outcome.
2. All participants must be prepared, be on time, have a positive attitude and be respectful.
3. At the end of the meeting, the outcome should be confirmed, action points with deadlines agreed and assigned.

Are meetings in your business meeting these criteria?

How can you minimise the time spent in meetings and the number of meetings, while achieving the desired outcomes for the business?

In conclusion, meetings are good indicators of the health of an organisation. The responsibility for managing and conducting meetings **is up to you**. They can be vehicles for desired and positive outcomes or, conversely, an opportunity to avoid responsibility and waste everybody's time and money.

2.3
TEAMWORK

2.3.1 Do people work for you or the business?

'People join companies. They leave managers.'[27]

Vern Harnish – founder of Young Entrepreneurs' Organisation and author

This is a great quote from Verne Harnish, author of *Scaling Up: How Few Companies Make it…and Most Don't.* I was talking to a former work colleague who was lamenting on the number of experienced long-term employees leaving his current employer. The managing director said it was because they did not like the new business owners. However, my former work colleague thought it was due to poor management.

As managers of people, we need to be conscious of how *our behaviour* and *performance* affects our subordinates. In my working life, I have never left a job because of the company – it was always because of my manager. A testament to this statement is that I got so sick of working for bad managers that I eventually went into running my own business so that I could have more control over my working life.

As a young graduate, I was thrown into the role of personnel officer in a steelworks department. I'd been forced onto the mill superintendent because of his poor record of industrial conflict and

---

27   Verne Harnish, *Scaling Up: How a Few Companies Make It..and why the Rest Don't,* Gezelles, 2014

poor workplace relationships. His first words to me were, 'I don't want you here, I could spend your salary in better ways.'

So, you can imagine the atmosphere in the department. His managers, supervisors and staff hated him as he was rude, uncommunicative, moody and difficult. I witnessed him causing a labour strike by abusing staff.

Another manager I worked for spent his time checking that his subordinates' petty cash and phone bills were correct. This was more important than visiting customers, developing his managers or building the business. The final straw came when the business was in the process of attempting to purchase a competitor. As always, he was too busy to discuss the negotiation strategy and, as a sign of complete incompetence, he did not even bring a pen to the final negotiations. Years later, he was dismissed – however, I had long left the business.

So, what causes good employees to quit?

The problem is generally with managers. It is seldom the employee or the quality of the workforce that causes employees to quit.

Do managers deliberately set out to be poor people-managers?

The answer, in most cases, is *'no'*.

Many managers have never been taught *the art of developing people* and *being a leader*. Often, they know no better – and, in some organisations, surviving means mimicking your old boss or their superiors.

In my experience there are **three main reasons** why people leave organisations:

1.　An employee's *contributions are not recognised*.
    As a manager, you should never underestimate the power of praise and recognising a job well done. Top performers are normally self-motivated. Don't take their drive for granted.

2. A manager *does not care about their subordinates.*
   This normally manifests itself in poor bosses. Research
   has shown that more than half of people who leave their
   jobs do so because of their relationship with their boss.

3. A manager *does not honour their commitments.*
   This highlights two traits required by managers: honesty
   and integrity. If you say you will do something – do it.
   Keeping your word tells the employee everything they
   need to know about the type of person you are and if
   they can trust you.

Surprisingly, salaries and conditions are not top of the list.

There are other reasons for leaving an organisation such as failing to develop employees, not challenging them, tolerating disruptive
employees and not acting on poor performance. Good employees
know who the poor performers are, and when poor performers leave,
morale improves [28].

If all else fails, remember: as business advisor and motivational
speaker Donn Carr says, *'People work for people – they do not work for
businesses.'* [29]

What are the warning signs?
Do you have high or unacceptable levels of employee turnover?

If so, could it be your management of your staff or other managers
are the cause?

Note: Some labour turnover is healthy, as it provides opportunities for new people, ideas and skills to come to the organisation.

---

28 See Chapter 2: People, section 3: Teamwork, part 4: What is the effect of
    disruptive employees in the workplace?

29 www.linkedin.com/pulse/people-work-people-they-do-business-
    donn-carr-nilda-alejandro

2.3.2 What's the difference between disruptive and unpredictable leadership?

'We have to be unpredictable.'[30]

Donald Trump – US President

In the media, we often hear about disruptive technology changing our lives and the workplace, for example, Uber disrupting the cosy taxi industry, or Amazon shaking up the retail industry. Disruptive technology is not new. Motor cars and railways disrupted horse-drawn transport.

Recently I was speaking to a good friend about his current work situation. Having known him for over 20 years, I was disturbed to hear his normally positive and enthusiastic voice very subdued and hesitant. It was not a pleasant conversation. However, my friend's story was different. The disrupter was not technology, but his unpredictable boss.

Unpredictable managers are not organisational psychopaths[31] and are more easily identified. Although they may engage in manipulative behaviour behind the scenes, a large proportion of their behaviour is clearly visible to their work colleagues and subordinates.

While some companies need to have disruptive leaders to provide positive direction and leadership to break out of their inertia or poor performance, **unpredictable leadership is a different** story.

This boss's behaviour was unpredictable and disruptive in a negative way. Meetings were arranged that had no planned agenda, team members were ridiculed in meetings and the goal posts were

---

30 Speech by Donald Trump, US President in April 2016
31 See Chapter 2: People, section 3: Teamwork, part 3: Can you recognise an organisational psychopath?

often unclear and seemed to keep changing. This unpredictability created a lot of 'noise' in the workplace. None of this was helpful as much time was wasted by team members struggling to work out how to navigate his leadership while trying to predict what he wanted. It became clear that this was a strategy to hide his lack of understanding of the business or industry and his lack of emotional intelligence, empathy and maturity, under the guise of 'keeping people on their toes'.

He was quoted as saying, 'I like to keep my subordinates on their toes because just when they think they have got me figured out, they realise they haven't.'

Time was wasted as the team spent unnecessary hours dealing with the fallout of working in an unstable and unpredictable environment. The environment was one of uncertainty, fear and mistrust. This created a culture of unhelpful and destructive game-playing. The best staff began leaving the company, profitability dropped, and customer service suffered. His behaviour was both unpredictable and disruptive in a negative way. The opposite of this behaviour is having a consistent style and track record, which people can learn to trust. In other words, being authentic.

US President Donald Trump, although a political disrupter to the established order, displays the characteristics of an unpredictable leader. His tweets and outbursts are unpredictable and often abusive, while appearing to play games and gamble with the fates of others.

Dealing with an unpredictable manager is certainly a challenge as it is *exhausting – both physically and mentally*. This was how my friend was feeling. The previous feelings of safety and being part of a team under the previous management were lost.

So, how do you deal with unpredictable managers?

Here are some suggestions:

- *Try and ignite empathy.*
  This is a challenge when being faced daily with unreasonable behaviours. However, if you try to think about why the person is acting this way, it can be beneficial for you both. People bring all sorts of baggage from their past. While having empathy does not condone unreasonable behaviour, it can help in trying to manage the situation. I can remember being confronted with unacceptable behaviour from a manager. However, when I considered that the person had suffered a recent family tragedy, it helped me deal with the situation better by depersonalising the behaviour.

- *Make a decision.*
  The decision is whether you are able to continue to tolerate the difficult situation. Ask yourself some questions to clarify your options:
  Is it impacting adversely on my life?
  If so, how much?
  What can I control and what is outside of my control?
  Is there someone I can ask to help me?
  For example, if the situation is affecting your health or personal relationships and you cannot control the situation, you may decide to leave the organisation or seek professional assistance.

- *What are your professional or personal boundaries?*
  Good employees and managers have clear boundaries, both personally and professionally. The issue of sexual harassment in the entertainment industry is a good example. Certain behaviour is unacceptable, and if your professional and personal boundaries are breached, then you probably should consider a plan to exit.

- *Seek perspective.*

  Often, we get emotionally involved in such situations so seeking an outside perspective can be an important step. When I was faced with unacceptable behaviour, I sought out an outside advisor or mentor to try and take the emotion out of the situation. However, it took me some time to undertake this course of action. This was after much emotional anguish, which was impacting on my family. I eventually left the organisation. It was liberating.

In conclusion, it is essential that you seek out some *clear-thinking time.*

Some suggestions include taking a walk around the block, visiting the gym or making notes in a journal so you can reflect. Such actions help you from becoming overwhelmed and you can go through the suggested steps in dealing with your *unpredictable and therefore disruptive manager.*

As managers, we have all witnessed disruptive behaviour by others in managing people and organisations. The challenge is to recognise such behaviour and use it for positive outcomes that benefit others, rather than derailing and decimating people and the organisation.

The decision is, as always, 'How can I manage the current unsatisfactory situation to make it positive?'

Both Asian and African elephants can be ridden by humans

2.3.3 Can you recognise an organisational psychopath?

'There's an absolute lack of conscience, lack of remorse,
and lack of guilt. They're manipulative, superficially charming,
and pathological liars. They like conning people and there's
a grandiose sense of self-importance.' [32]

Dr John Clarke – expert on work psychopaths

The news media has been full of stories of inappropriate and unacceptable behaviour by men in powerful positions. Alleged sleazy and bullying behaviour from toxic workers are certainly topical.

Toxic employees can have a detrimental effect on an organisation. Failure to act can be costly in terms of morale and profits, and it also takes away the positive energy required for managing an organisation.

One form of the toxic employee is the 'organisational psychopath' [33].

The term psychopath conjures up images of evil murderers from Hollywood movies such as Hannibal Lector in *The Silence of the Lambs*. However, they generally don't murder people. Instead, they destroy work colleagues and their subordinates, as well as seriously damaging the organisations they work for.

Have you ever worked with or for an organisational psychopath? How do you recognise one?

They are not normally the overbearing, rude and unreasonable boss. They are far too clever for that and often remain undetected for years in organisations.

Years ago, I worked for one. He was superficially charming, had excellent oral communication skills, was outwardly extremely

---

32   James Adonis, 'Beware the workplace psychopath' *The Sydney Morning Herald*,
     8 April 2011

33   https://www.forbes.com/sites/victorlipman/2013/04/25/the-disturbing-link-
     between-psychopathy-and-leadership/#66034ff84104

confident and 'managed up' exceptionally well. All traits of an organisational psychopath.

Within three months, without my knowledge, he was wanting to dismiss me. There were no conversations about performance and he certainly gave me no assistance in my role. I later found out that he had previously forced the departure of several other employees. What alerted me was him undermining and subtly criticising the staff under my control. He was known as the 'the smiling assassin' and was displaying the psychopathic characteristics of *lack of conscience*.

My wife came to work to pick me up one afternoon with our six-month-old baby. He was dismissive and rude. This should have rung alarm bells, as one of the characteristics of a psychopath is a *lack of empathy*.

He was described as a hero by the business owner. Under his supervision, using new technology, the business had grown significantly in terms of profit and revenue. I found out later that another executive was instrumental in advising and assisting him in implementing the new technology, and opened the doors with existing customers. This shows two other characteristics of organisational psychopaths – *claiming credit for others work* and being *manipulative*.

Like all good organisational psychopaths, he left the organisation before he was found out. Upon leaving, the final confirmation fell into place. I was to complete a project he had commenced and found some of the stages had not been completed as he claimed. Yes, the final characteristic was being a *pathological liar*.

The experience of working for this organisational psychopath left me somewhat scarred. I lost my confidence and felt demoralised. However, I learnt how to recognise organisational psychopathic behaviour and made a pact with myself never to work with or for one again, and to help others cope who had been affected by their behaviour.

The characteristics of an organisational psychopath are:

- Superficially charming
- Outwardly confident
- Always manage up
- Manipulative
- Lack of conscience
- Lack of empathy
- Claiming credit for others' work
- Pathological liars.

Would you be able to recognise one?

2.3.4 What is the effect of disruptive employees in the workplace?

'If you accept the expectations of others, especially negative ones, then you never will change the outcome.'[34]

Michael Jordan – professional basketballer

Have you ever worked with or for a person who is disruptive?

Was it always about them and not about the team?

Workplaces are strange social environments. We are thrown together with those who we would not normally choose to spend time with. Having said that, it is our responsibility to work as hard as we can to make our relationships at work productive, to perform our jobs to the best of our ability, and to help ensure the organisation and the careers of those within the organisation are successful.

---

34 Attributed to Michael Jackson, US basketball player and principal team owner of the Charlotte Hornets

Disruptive employees display the following characteristics at work:

- They constantly see the negative points of issues –
  the glass is half empty.
- They try to get others onto 'their side'.
- They turn minor inconveniences into major ones,
  often in loud voices and with great drama.
- They come up with complicated explanations
  for the most simple occurrences.
- They never meet deadlines.
- They bore people with their social lives often to
  the extent of what they had for dinner.
- Are often away sick more than other employees.

We, as managers, are often paralysed by indecision when confronted with employees who disrupt the work environment and the performance of the team or business.

Why is this?
Probably because we prefer to *make life easier for ourselves by not confronting the problem.*

Are we really making it easier for ourselves? I doubt that there is any manager in the world who can honestly say that they have not deferred confronting the problem. I have certainly been guilty of this. Can you remember when a disruptive employee left an organisation?

Everybody in the team breathed a sigh of relief and became more productive again.

I remember working with a disruptive employee who was always sick. Everything was a drama, she was negative and dismissive of new ideas, and she disrupted fellow workmates who were too polite to tell her to 'go away' – boring them with her love life and what she cooked for dinner each evening. When she left, there was an enormously positive change in the work environment.

So, what can we learn from this?

1. *Teams look for leadership.*
    As the manager, you have the **authority to act in ways that benefit the team**.

    In another instance, a state manager we employed was harassing and threatening staff while telling one of the directors each afternoon what a great job he was doing. The financial results did not show this. His subordinates were demoralised and were seeking support. A window of opportunity presented itself. We had proof that company policy had been seriously violated and, with the director out of the country, we sacked the manager. The relief from his direct supports was immediate. They stopped looking for work outside the company and their morale improved overnight.

2. *True leadership improves a company's performance.*
    In another example, the holding company of a business I was advising was struggling to achieve their profit and sales targets. Disruptive and difficult staff distracted senior management. They decided to bite the bullet and take action by introducing what they called a 'no d%ckhead policy' (NDP). Initially, it was difficult. However, as the disruptive staff were encouraged to leave the business, the company's position improved significantly and they became the leader in their market niche, increasing sales and profits well above budget.

3. *Disruptive employees cost money, either directly or indirectly.*
It's your duty as a manager to manage and not abdicate
this essential activity. Your team is watching you. **Either
manage them and have a plan to ensure acceptable
behaviour or manage them out of the business.** You
owe it to your staff and customers. As with the previous
example, when management enforced accepted standards
of behaviour and performance both morale and profits
improved.

Are there disruptive employees in your business?

Are they affecting the performance of your department or
business?

What are *you going to do about it?*

2.3.5 Being late. Is it good business etiquette?

*'Etiquette means behaving yourself a little better than is
absolutely essential.'* [35]

Will Cuppy – American humourist and literary critic

Manners are about respect for other people, whether in business or in
a social setting. It is not old-fashioned to have good manners. It has
nothing to do with 'fashion' or 'generation'.

Is it OK to be late for a meeting or an appointment?

Too often in business, people run late for meetings and, when
they arrive, are often ill-prepared. They think nothing of drifting into
a meeting, five, 10 or 15 minutes after starting time.

Professional managers do not find this acceptable.

---

35   Will Cuppy, *How to Become Extinct*, Farrer & Rinehart, 1941

I was recently at a meeting where six people were kept waiting in a meeting for 20 minutes until one team member idled their way in, unprepared and 20 minutes late. That equals six people times 20 minutes wasted each or 120 minutes wasted. Yes, two hours wasted.

How much has that cost the business?

The best thing to do to prevent this wastage is to start the meeting without them. They are unlikely to be late next time.

Although cost is a factor, it is the **lack of respect** for the other people in the meeting that is also important. Whether you are their manager or the business owner is *not relevant*.

This lack of respect can flow through the whole organisation and it can tell you a lot about the values being promoted within an organisation.

There are other actions in meetings that are NOT acceptable and show lack of respect:

1. Making and taking phone calls during a meeting – both rude and disrespectful
2. Checking emails or texts during a meeting
3. Not being prepared.

If you can't give the meeting your time, don't attend. It is as simple as that.

This manifests itself in other ways. Failure to return phone calls or reply to emails is just plain rude. It is like someone saying good morning to you and you ignoring them. In my experience, most of the people who are late for meetings are generally the same people who are not prepared for meetings, and who check their texts and take and make phone calls during the meeting.

With important meetings, I always try to be five minutes early just in case there is a problem. If you are unavoidably late, call or text 15 minutes before the scheduled time. **It's good manners and also shows respect**. Much more can be achieved when you show respect. If you show respect, in most cases it will be returned – not only making your job easier but achieving a constructive outcome for the business.

Before I went into business, I worked for a business owner who was extremely successful and wealthy. He always opened the door for you, allowing you to enter and leave first and was never late for meetings. Even when we had company team gym sessions, he always made sure he was the last person to take a shower. It goes without saying he was highly respected and managed an exceptionally successful business.

We all lead 'busy' lives. It's a cop-out to use that as an excuse. Do you really think that your time is more important than someone else's? [36]

Apparently, much of the success achieved by Nelson Mandela in finally toppling apartheid in South Africa was his ability to treat everybody with respect, including his prison guards on Robben Island. In a TV documentary program I watched on Mandela, he was described as always giving people his undivided attention and time, which made people feel valued and important. In this documentary, there was a section graphically showing Mandela publicly chastising the then-president Thabo Mbeke when he showed a lack of respect by arriving late to a meeting he was to address where Mandela was also a guest of honour.

Remember **good etiquette and manners pays off**...

Are you, as a business owner or manager, showing people adequate respect?

---

36   see Chapter 2: People, section 2: Management, part 6: Who's managing the meeting?

2.3.6 Can you manage your destructive emotions?

'If your emotional abilities aren't in hand, if you don't have self-awareness, if you are not able to manage your distressing emotions, if you can't have empathy and have effective relationships, then no matter how smart you are, you are not going to get very far.'[37]

Daniel Goleman – originator of the term 'emotional intelligence'

Does expressing your emotions openly in business help serve your goals or your company's goals?

In my opinion, it depends on what emotions you are expressing and whether they are negative or positive.

Many years ago, upon finding out that my manager had sacked a colleague, I confronted him. I believed his actions were unjustifiable and were to cover up his own incompetence and failures. On display were *my negative emotions which are destructive and debilitating*. It was not a wise action. It showed my lack of control and self-awareness, and these actions indicated that I was not management material either. Furthermore, I didn't know if burning this bridge would have negative impacts for me in the future.

Do you really think that your bridge-burning, fire-breathing rant is going to change things and that company management will suddenly come to their senses?

No.

I learnt from this mistake and vowed to hold my tongue and display more self-awareness and professionalism in the future.

Years later, I experienced a similar situation when two managers were using me as a scapegoat for the business not performing

37 Daniel Goleman, *Emotional Intelligence*, Bloomsbury Publishing, 1996

and they were recommending my termination. Upon hearing this, I decided on a positive approach rather than being confrontational and burning my bridges.

Positive emotions are liberating and invigorating. Think of people you work with who are positive and enthusiastic. They get things done. People follow them. People like working for them – they are leaders.

Luckily, I had built up constructive relationships with others in the company and with clients, and my position was saved while they were forced from the business. Less than three years later, one of them came to me with a very large potential customer for our own logistics business. We were successful in securing this customer and it helped underpin the business and form a foundation for the business to grow.

This business-saving opportunity would not have happened if I had burnt my bridges...

Do you think before you act emotionally?

2.3.7 What is Koala Bear Syndrome©?

'...flea-ridden, piddling, stinking, scratching, rotten little things...'[38]
John Brown – Australian Minister for Sport, Recreation and Tourism

In the 1980s, the Minister for Sport, Recreation and Tourism, John Brown, sparked a national outcry when he described the koala bear in such a disparaging way. Koalas are considered a national animal icon in Australia and a favourite with overseas tourists. Koalas are not actually bears, they are mammal marsupials (have pouches) and are protected by law.

---

38   As quoted in an article by Misha Schubert, "House on the Hill" in *The Age*, 19 June 2008

Koalas are found in the eucalyptus forests of eastern Australia and feast exclusively on eucalyptus leaves, which are tough and not very nutritious. They are covered in grey fur, weigh up to 14 kilograms, have strong clawed feet suitable for climbing and living in trees, and are universally considered 'cute'. Their poor diet means that they get little energy and need to eat up to one kilogram of leaves per day while being very docile and sleeping up to 18 hours per day. The koala's brain is very small, and they are considered the least intelligent mammal in the world. In summary, the koala is protected, considered 'cute', not very intelligent, docile and not very productive.

The concept of the **Koala Bear Syndrome©** (KBS©) has been developed from a lifetime of work experiences in a range of businesses. Fellow workers often referred to some of their peers, colleagues and bosses as 'marsupials'.

They didn't have pouches, so why call them marsupials?

Because, like most marsupials in Australia, they appeared to be a *protected species* and displayed such characteristics as being chronic underperformers who could say and do anything without bearing the consequences or being held accountable. However, I consider the characteristics of the koala a better description of such people – particularly those who produce little, underperform, lack energy, are lazy, continually make the same mistakes, are incompetent and, more importantly, appear to be protected by their managers. They are rarely held to account. Koalas are another form of the disruptive employee, although they are likely to be less obvious[39].

Sadly, few organisations are completely free from KBS©. We all have our blind spots[40] and the challenge is to be self-aware enough to

---

39   See Chapter 2: People, section 3: Teamwork, part 4: What is the effect of disruptive employees in the workplace?

40   See Chapter 4: Processes, section 2: Methods, part 3: Can see but am blind?

recognise them. Looking back, there are times when I have allowed KBS© to exist by failing to recognise it. KBS© *tends to manifest itself more in private family companies* – where business owners are more emotionally involved and where family members are not held to the same standards as other employees[41]. Employing relatives and friends is also another area where KBS© is more likely exist.

Are there koalas in your organisation?

How do you recognise them and what are you going to about it?

Value statements, structured performance appraisals, codes of conduct[42] and clear and strong leadership can assist in managing KBS©.

2.3.8 Christmas is coming...again

'What I don't like about office Christmas parties is looking for a job the next day.'[43]

Phyllis Diller – American comedian

Despite Christmas being a time of joy and celebration, it can also be, unfortunately, a disaster for both businesses and staff. Every year, we hear stories of work Christmas parties that go wrong – drunkenness, inappropriate and embarrassing behaviour, work accidents, and the like. Often management or the organisation is blamed for the outcomes. It's even more disappointing when it is traditionally a period of cheer and goodwill.

---

41 See Chapter 6: Profits, section 3: Dangers, part 1: What are the dangers for profitability with family businesses?

42 See Chapter 3: Planning, section 1: Framework, part 3: Business values – are they of value?

43 Gyles Brandreth, *Messing About with Quotes*, Oxford University Press, 2018

So, what should you, as a manager or business owner, do to protect yourself and your staff from a bad outcome at Christmas?

What are the 'rules'?
The rules need to be clearly defined and communicated. For example, refer to your organisation's code of conduct and values[44]. Managing the serving of alcohol is important and, as part of the leadership team, you must be present and be a role model.

What are the aims?
Christmas parties should be about more than having fun. It's a good time to reflect on achievements of the business and the staff. This should obviously come from the most senior manager – whether the CEO, owner or department manager. It's a time to display leadership, celebrate your business and your staff's achievements, and to thank them for their efforts. It is also an opportunity to set the tone for next year.

What are you planning for your work Christmas party that will achieve these aims?

The islands of Crete and Sicily were once the home to a species of miniature 'dwarf' elephants

---

44   See Chapter 3: Planning, section 1: Framework, part 6: Codes of conduct

3
PLANNING

The second 'P' in the five dimensions of improving business performance is planning. Planning cannot be done in isolation and needs a framework and solid foundations. The dilemma, once you have gathered a team around you to assist you in eating the elephant, is how will you cook it? Cooking five tonnes of the world's largest land mammal needs planning.

Who will be sharing in the feast? When will it be eaten? How much will everybody get to eat? Will some of the meat need to be preserved and stored after cooking? What is the best method of cooking: the pot, on a barbeque or in a pit? What do we do with the inedible parts of the elephant?

These are big dilemmas that are best handled in small manageable bites. A plan of action or roadmap with clear goals underpinned by values is required. Selling ivory is illegal. However, the hide can be tanned and made into leather goods and the feet into umbrella stands. How and who do we communicate the plan to? How and what do we need to communicate so eating the elephant is successful?

3.1
FRAMEWORK

3.1.1 Visualising your goals

'If I could have seen France, I would have made it.'[1]
Francis Chadwick – long-distance swimmer

Francis Chadwick was the first woman to swim the English Channel in both directions. She failed in her first attempt after spending 14 hours in the water. This attempt was made in thick fog and, ironically, she was only three miles from France when she abandoned her attempted crossing.

There are few better examples of the importance of setting goals and *visualising* those goals. Several years ago, I was trekking in the McDonnell Ranges near Alice Springs in central Australia. Not only was it an amazing visual experience but it was also a time to reflect and enjoy the company of interesting people, as well as a physical challenge. Each day we set out to walk the 18-20km in a harsh desert environment. *This meant setting goals for the day* – how far to walk by what time.

On our second day, we got up at 5:30 am and trekked 8km through a gorge, over rocky and steep terrain, onto open spinifex-covered slopes, to the summit of Mount Sonder. This mountain was one of

---

1   Attributed comments to Francis Chadwick in attempting to swim the English Channel but it most likely occurred when she attempted to swim from Catalina Island to California in 1952.

the highest points on the Larapinta Trail, with 180-degree views for over 100km of the surrounding country. At times, it was physically quite difficult. However, it was made easier as we had one goal. We could see the mountain in front of us. Unlike Francis Chadwick's first attempt at swimming the English Channel, we could see our goal and kept going. The magnificent views were one of the rewards for our efforts.

Everybody should have goals – whether it's to obtain a degree, learn a new skill, be financially independent, buy your first home or start a business.

Without clear goals, you are less likely to achieve your potential – or anything else, for that matter. Too few of us set goals in life or in our work. Importantly, by not having *written goals*, we are even less likely to achieve our potential.

A quote from Lewis Carroll's *Alice in Wonderland* explains the situation clearly, *'If you don't know where you are going, any road can take you there.'*[2]

I have found that, although writing down goals is important, it is critical that you also have a plan with milestones to help you meet your goals. In climbing Mount Sonder, we had location milestones to reach by set times to ensure we climbed it in the time planned, and to complete our descent before the heat of the afternoon set in.

In conclusion, an often-overlooked part of goal setting is to *visualise* your goal. I have found that visualising the completed goal is a powerful motivator.

In selling our business[3], I visualised what it would be like to finally be rewarded for all that hard work. A bit like climbing Mount Sonder, where we visualised the spectacular views and enjoying

---

2   Lewis Carroll, *Alice's Adventures in Wonderland, 1865*
3   See Chapter 6: Profits, section 1: Measures, part 1: Exit strategy...

a well-earned rest. To be able to see the mountain helped. Francis Chadwick, in her second and successful attempt at swimming the English Channel, could see the English shore.

Can you *visualise* what the completion of *your goals* looks like?

3.1.2 Vision

'I believe that this Nation should commit itself to achieving the goal, before this decade is out, of landing a man on the moon and returning him safely to earth.'[4]

John F. Kennedy – former US President

This quote, delivered in 1961 by President Kennedy, is one of the best examples of a vision statement. Within the decade, man had landed on the moon and returned safely. On 20th July 1969, astronauts Armstrong and Aldrin landed on the moon and returned safely to earth, fulfilling Kennedy's vision. However, it is important to remember that the moon landing was the result of decades of work by hundreds of thousands of people, working across the disciplines of science, technology, and engineering – peaking at a cost of 4.41% of the US federal budget in 1966.

How important is it for an organisation to have a vision?
A vision is a picture or an idea. It helps focus us on the future, provides inspiration and assists in overcoming the obstacles that inevitably appear along the way. A vision is a target. It should be aspirational, perhaps like the concept of a BHAG (Big Hairy Audacious Goal) in Jim Collins' *Built to Last: Successful Habits of Visionary Companies* and be successfully communicated throughout the organisation.

---

4   Speech by John F Kennedy, US President to Congress on 25 May 1961.

An example of the power of an aspirational vision is Rotary International's PolioPlus program. In 1979 Clement 'Clem' Renouf, the Australian president of Rotary International, read in the *Reader's Digest Magazine* how smallpox had been eradicated. After discussing this with a medical expert, he had a vision that the world could be polio-free. At the time, more than 350,000 people were infected by polio in 125 countries each year. Later that year, Rotary International's board of directors passed a resolution for a program for 'the eradication of poliomyelitis and the alleviation of its consequences' throughout the world. Subsequently, in 1985 the PolioPlus program was adopted with the aim of eradicating polio worldwide. With so many countries where polio was still endemic, this was a challenging vision.

Rotary initiated the program, and together with the support of UNICEF, WHO and other organisations such as the Bill and Melinda Gates Foundation, have almost achieved Clem Renouf's original vision. By 2018, only 33 cases of polio were reported in just two countries: Afghanistan and Pakistan. At times, there were difficulties in overcoming cultural suspicion and low levels of education, training staff to manage and administer the program, political insurgencies and geographical remoteness. However, despite these obstacles, the original vision ensured the program continued. It is now almost complete.

There are many websites and other sources who provide a methodology on how to create a vision statement for your organisation. As can be demonstrated from the above two examples, strong and clear visions are powerful tools and can provide a framework for the future. Visions should be compiled into a vision statement in a suitable form to communicate to staff, customers, suppliers and other stakeholders. Vision statements define goals and assist in creating a path for the future.

Does your organisation have a vision statement?

If not, do you think that the organisation *would benefit* from having a vision statement?

President Kennedy's and Clem Renouf's visions are great examples of the impact of having a vision statement.

3.1.3 Business values - are they of value?

'When you are led by values, it doesn't cost your business, it helps your business.'[5]

Jerry Greenfield – co-founder of Ben & Jerry's and philanthropist

Many advisers and media commentators maintain that business values are essential for a business to be successful. *Many CEOs and business owners think this is 'consultant speak' or a marketing ploy to drum up business.* They think the prime purpose of business is to make money. If this was the case, perhaps the illegal drug business would meet this criterion.

An ongoing debate in the business sector seems to be around whether business values are of any value at all.

When Moses received the 10 Commandments on Mount Sinai, what was their purpose? To give clear expectations on how God expected people to behave and dictate what someone of the Jewish faith can and cannot do.

So, in our modern world, has anything changed?

Are values in business important?

Think of some recent business failures. These may illustrate the point about whether values are important. Remember the Enron scandal in

---

5   Attributed to Jerry Greenfield, co-founder of Ben & Jerry's ice cream

2001 where the company defrauded investors and the senior executives were jailed? What about the late Alan Bond, winner of the 1983 America's Cup, who deceptively siphoned off shareholders' funds from the Bell Group to prop up his Bond Corporation in the 1990s? Unfortunately, not only were shareholders' funds lost. People also lost their jobs.

Wayne Bennett, an Australian National Rugby League (NRL) coach is a positive example of the **'value of values'** in an organisation. In over 25 years of first-grade coaching, his teams have won seven premierships. Quietly spoken, at times appearing unemotional, much of Bennett's success could be attributed to his high values, which flow onto the players in the teams he coaches.

Talent is not enough. Players who did not meet behavioural standards and work ethics or did not have the team's interests at heart were quickly removed from the team. Bennett showed his true values when he sacked the captain of both the Broncos and the Australian Rugby League team, Wally Lewis. The public outcry was overwhelming. Irate fans called for the Broncos to reinstate Lewis and sack Bennett. But Bennett had the long-term interests of the club at heart and the Broncos went on to win more premierships.

As a manager or business owner, **business values** and **your values** are important. Sound business values lead to better workplaces, more satisfied customers and higher profits. Furthermore, they provide guidance on how to handle everyday problems. *Therefore, values have expectations.*

What are your personal values?
Does your organisation have a **value statement**, and do **they live these values**?

As a manager or business owner, people whether employees, customers or the public are watching...

3.1.4 Are all your eggs in the one basket?

'Don't put all your eggs in one basket.'
Anonymous

I love travelling. Travelling allows me to experience unique cultures, see beautiful and interesting sights and, most importantly, meet interesting people. It's amazing what you can *learn from listening* to other people's experiences.

On an aeroplane trip to Zimbabwe, I was fortunate to be sitting next to a local businessman who was returning home from South Africa. In conversation, he gave me his family's life story. He had several businesses and some urban property assets. and was managing to survive despite the severe economic circumstances. His family once owned several farms, employing hundreds of people. With the encouragement of the government, these farms were 'taken over' by so-called 'war veterans' in the early 2000s with no compensation. In other words, his farms were stolen, and thousands lost their jobs.

Apart from the obvious injustice, his position emphasised an important strategy for business owners. I had initially seen this strategy used by a former employer.

The strategy was **'don't put all your eggs in one basket'**

Unlike many farmers who had lost their farms in the 'farm invasions,' the Zimbabwean businessman had survived because he had *diversified his businesses*, thereby protecting his wealth. Likewise, my former employer had carefully separated his business into various categories – operating business, fixed assets, property and stock exchange investments. If the operating business failed, then the rest of his wealth was not threatened.

The lessons learnt from my former employer were implemented in our business. This could not have been done without a *very disciplined approach*, as at times our business struggled. We invested a proportion of our profits into an investment portfolio outside the operating business. When we sold the business, the investments had grown threefold.

Too often, I have seen business owners draw out funds from their business for private use such as expensive cars, children's school fees and overseas holidays – and then get into trouble with the tax office and creditors when the business struggles financially.

Have you got *'all your eggs in the one basket'*?

If you have, perhaps you need to **reassess** your situation…

3.1.5 What are the foundations of a good business?

'You can't build a great building on a weak foundation. You must have a solid foundation if you're going to have a strong superstructure.'[6]

Gordon B. Hinckley – American religious leader

Deciding to go into business is the first step. The second step is to ensure that, from the beginning, the business has **solid foundations**. This is critical and relevant whether your business is a start-up, or you are purchasing an existing business. Like a building constructed on solid rock, a business with a solid foundation will have a better chance of surviving the *inevitable challenges* than one built on unstable foundations. Cracks will inevitably appear in a business over time, as they do in a building. By solid foundations, I don't mean a market niche, systems and processes, skilled employees and loyal customers – such instructions can be easily found in 'how to' management books, and on the internet.

---

6   https://gordonhinckley.com/about

When my partners and I were going into business, it involved a management buyout of an unprofitable business. We were eager to 'have a go' on our own and prove we could build a successful business. This leap of faith meant mortgaging our houses to raise the capital – not an unusual practice for funding new businesses. This certainly focussed our attention. Failure could mean losing the family home and all the implications associated with family life.

As with an elephant's legs supporting the world's largest land animal, having a solid foundation on which to build and support a business is essential. Luckily, the previous owner had an excellent financial director who provided us with some practical and useful advice:

'Protect your assets and limit your risks and liabilities'.

We also sought advice from external experts. As owners and managers, we **didn't know what we didn't know**. Seeking external expertise is essential. From our experience in setting up in business, external assistance is required in the following disciplines:

1. *Legal advice* in setting up the business's legal entities (including each owner's private company, which was also a shareholder in the business), establishing corporate structures that reduce the exposure to legal claims from avaricious ambulance-chasing lawyers, completing shareholders' agreements, terms and conditions and suppliers' agreements.

   One of the lessons learnt was that, while the structure of the founding team set out the entitlements of each founder, we did not clearly outline our roles and responsibilities. This led to performance and accountability issues and was complicated by two family tragedies. This could have been managed more effectively if roles and responsibilities had been more clearly set out and if we had established a company board that held the executive team and founders to account.

2.   *Financial advice* from a chartered accountant on business-related finance issues, including insurance, taxation, banking and recommended corporate structure, in combination with legal advice[7]. The essential lesson learnt was to separate the business entity from personal affairs. Unfortunately, I have witnessed some businesses getting into financial difficulty by not separating private and business affairs – as well as a lack of discipline and no clear understanding of the importance of keeping this separate. This is particularly relevant to family businesses[8].

3.   *Strategic business advice* from an advisor with business-owner experience. There are two issues here:
     •   seeking external advice
     •   ensuring it comes from a consultant or advisor who has practical experience in managing and owning a business.

     Too often, there are consultants who do not have this experience and do not understand what it is like to have their money and house on the line.

     In retrospect, we should have sought external assistance in strategic planning for our logistics business.

---

7   See Chapter 3: Planning, section 1: Framework, part 7: Can you compare the game of cricket to business?

8   See Chapter 6: Profits, section 3: Dangers, part 1: What are the dangers for profitability with family businesses?

Our annual budgets were built from the ground up[9] and served as our business plan. The weaknesses became apparent in our lacking the vital areas of values, vision and a mission statement which underpin the budgets and business plan. We did not recognise their importance. The values, vision and mission statement were only created when we established a webpage. We would have benefited immensely from engaging an external advisor earlier in the piece. The business, although profitable, would have been more profitable and would have developed more strategically. Professional external advice would have opened up opportunities through identifying strategic long-term customers, obtaining government grants and developing new networks.

In conclusion, the message is to *seek advice from those with expertise*. Give the business solid foundations, so that when the inevitable storm comes, the business has a greater chance of survival. **Seeking external advice is not a sign of weakness.** Elite athletes and sporting teams all have coaches. A business is no different. Also, as a manager and business owner, *ongoing education is essential* for continual success[10].

---

9   See Chapter 6: Profits, section 1: Measures, part 4: Is an annual budget really that important?

10 See Chapter 3: Planning, section 3: Communication, part 6: Reading is not just for Christmas…

3.1.6 Codes of conduct

'Don't violate your own code of values and ethics, but don't waste energy trying to make other people violate theirs.'[11]

Melody Beattie – American self-help author

What is a code of conduct and is it important for a business?

A code of conduct is a set of rules or standards that capture the beliefs and ethics on behavioural expectations in the organisation. There are many types of business codes ranging from financial reporting, conflicts of interest, health and safety, and communication to employment discrimination. A code of conduct sets out a common standard of performance for employees, while respecting the rights of employees and providing a framework for acceptable behaviour.

One of the best examples of a code of conduct is Rotary International's Four-Way Test[12] for use in professional and personal relationships:

1. Is it the TRUTH?
2. Is it FAIR to all concerned?
3. Will it build GOODWILL and BETTER FRIENDSHIPS?
4. Will it be BENEFICIAL to all concerned?

Codes of conduct are linked to corporate or organisational values and the mission statement. A good demonstration of the use of

---

11   Attributed to Melody Beattie, US self-help author who introduced the term "co-dependency"

12   https://my.rotary.org/en/guiding-principles

corporate values as a guide for decision-making is this example from one of the transport companies I worked for:

'If you ask yourself the following five questions and you can answer 'yes' to all of them confidently, you should go ahead and make the decision:

- Will the decision help me exceed customer expectations?
- Is it respectful to all individuals – customers, suppliers, employees and community residents?
- Does it further our goal of continuous improvement?
- Is it in the long-term best financial interests of the company?
- Can I do it safely and ethically?'

If the answer to any of these questions is 'no', then the decision you are about to make is unacceptable.

The values, in the form of a card that could fit into a wallet, were given to all staff so they could be referred to when required.

In our logistics business, we had a values statement which was as follows:

'Customers and employees are our greatest assets. The company is committed to providing the highest level of service by working with its customers in an environment of continuous improvement through the introduction of new technology, superior systems, staff training and development.

Work performance and service quality is enhanced by giving responsibility to supervisors on the shop floor. The flat management structure drives the efficiency and effectiveness of the business. It has enabled the company to react quickly to opportunities and requests from current and potential customers.'

However, *the statement did not set out specific values driving organi-sational behaviour* – such as work standards, accountability, being open and fair, or personal interactions and behaviour. It did not summarise what needed to be done – for example, 'we will celebrate success and encourage initiative' – and what will not be done – for example, 'we will not tolerate poor performance or rude and condescending behaviour towards others'.

Why was this important?

Because we did not have these values clearly defined, we could not use it as a basis for managing interpersonal conflict when the business was struggling in one area. The failure to accept responsibility for continuing unacceptable performance by a senior manager[13] who was in denial[14], and not having a clear values statement, resulted in an acrimonious and deteriorating situation. Unfortunately, I did not manage the situation constructively at the time and, out of sheer frustration, I allowed my emotions[15] to override a common sense approach to resolving the situation satisfactorily for the business.

Conflicts within organisations are inevitable. The challenge is to manage conflicts when they arise in a constructive way.

Does your business have a code of conduct?

Does it clearly set out the *acceptable standards of behaviour* as well as a *framework to manage conflict*?

For example, does it say 'we will respect and support each other as individuals and members of the team and we will recognise both group and individual results' and 'we will not ignore achievements or tolerate poor performance'?

---

13 See Chapter 4: Processes, section 1: Essentials, part 1: Problems
14 See Chapter 2: People, section 2: Management, part 5: 'Denial is not a river in Egypt'
15 See Chapter 2: People, section 2: Teamwork, part 6: Can you manage your destructive emotions?

3.1.7 Can you compare the game of cricket to business?

'If there is any game in the world that attracts the half-baked theorist more than cricket I have yet to hear of it.'[16]

Fred Trueman – English cricketer

Think of the game of cricket. There are four main parties involved – the batting side, the fielding side, the umpires and the scorers.

Can running a business be compared to the game of cricket? Yes.

In business, you have *active participants* – employees and customers. In cricket, you have active participants that make things happen – the bowlers and fielders on one side and the batsmen on the other.

In business, you also have parties that are *not active in running the business* – chartered or compliance accountants, solicitors and government, including its instrumentalities. In cricket, you also have a party not active in the game of cricket – the scorers and umpires.

Do chartered accountants perform a similar role to scorers in cricket?

Scorers only record what is happening. They never give advice on what to do for the future or participate in the game.

What do accountants do?

They record what has happened *in the past*. They do not actively participate in the game of business. If chartered accountants offer business advice, I would caution against accepting such advice if they do not have business experience.

This may seem a harsh statement about chartered accountants but let me give you an example.

---

16   Fred Trueman, *Fred Trueman's Book of Cricket, Pelham Books, 1964*

The builder who performed some of our house renovations told me a story about his accountant which had severe ramifications. Over 10 years ago, his son set up a retail business. They both went to their accountant for 'professional advice' on how they should set up the legal entities for the business. His accountant came up with a corporate or business structure 'on the cheap', saving them $1,000 and making them joint directors of the new company and the existing building company.

After initially being very successful, the retail business failed. Due to the linkage between the two companies, the father became liable for the debts of the retail venture, pushing him to the brink of bankruptcy. In saving the initial $1,000 he nearly lost his house. The advice from their accountant was neither professional nor correct. It highlights *the risk of accountants calling themselves business or legal advisors*, especially as many have not actually run a business other than their accounting practice.

Receiving business or legal advice from a chartered accountant, as distinct from compliance accounting advice for taxation purposes is a risky strategy.

Do you go to a dentist if you have a sore back or a cold?

Then you should not go to a chartered accountant for legal or business advice, unless they have the necessary experience and qualifications. Our builder's accountant not only failed to give the correct professional advice, he also did not foresee what could happen if the business failed.

What are the lessons from this story?

Seek *professional advice* from those experts[17] with the *appropriate expertise and experience.*

Also in your personal life, seek advice from professionals in their field. It is less likely to put your business or your health at risk.

> Poaching, habitat loss and conflict with humans are the major threats to elephants

---

17 See Chapter 3: Planning, section 1: Framework, part 5: What are the foundations of a good business?

3.2
ROADMAP

3.2.1 Life cycle

'What Is a Product Life Cycle? Products, like people, have life cycles. The product life cycle is broken into four stages: introduction, growth, maturity, and decline'[18]

Definition from: Investopedia

Yes, we all know about product life cycles. Just look at how car manufacturers redesign car styles. Business leaders and business owners have a life cycle too. *The issue is knowing where you are in your career or business life cycle and then planning and acting accordingly.*

CEOs of family businesses have great difficulty in 'letting go'. The issue is often an emotional one. Many business owners have invested so much time and money in working long hours that they see stepping down as being 'put out to pasture'. Ego, loss of self-worth, so-called Relevance Deprivation Syndrome (RDS) which retiring politicians claim they suffer from, and perceived lifestyle all play a part.

Great leaders know when it's time to pass the baton. Former Australian Liberal prime minister John Howard refused to hand over the leadership to his deputy, Peter Costello. The result was a lost election in 2007, with Costello leaving politics, Howard losing his seat and the Liberal party having five leaders over the next 12 years.

---

18   https://www.investopedia.com/terms/p/product-life-cycle.asp

All businesses must have a succession plan.

There are two types of succession plans: short-term or emergency succession plans – the 'what happens if you are hit by a bus?' scenario[19], and long-term succession plans which protect your company's culture, value and future.

If you are a family-owned business, you owe it to your family, employees and customers to have a well planned and executed succession plan. It is not a sign of weakness but of strength, and you will be recognised for it. I have seen too many companies suffer when they do not have succession plan or have a poor one. Inevitably a succession plan will be needed.

There is no greater satisfaction than mentoring and training a replacement successfully. If you do not plan for your succession, then you have failed as a leader and have failed your business.

Start planning now...

Where you are in your career and business life cycle?

When should you start succession planning?

3.2.2 Business plan – why the journey is more important than the destination?

'A goal without a plan is just a wish.'[20]

Antoine de Saint-Exupéry – French writer and pioneering aviator

What is a business plan?

It is a formal statement of future business goals and a plan for reaching those goals.

---

19 See Chapter 3: Planning, section 2: Roadmap, part 8: Business continuity – do you have a plan?

20 Attributed to Antoine de Saint-Exupery French poet, author and fighter pilot killed in World War II

In their 2017/18 SME Research Report, Australian financial and business advisory HLB Mann Judd found a staggering four in five businesses did not have a working business plan. Of those with a business plan, only one in three regularly spent time refining their plan. Similar results were found in the UK in 2015 in a survey by Barclays Bank. Only 47% of all UK small- to medium-sized enterprises (SMEs) had a formal written business plan.

Should this be of concern? Yes.

Failing to plan increases the likelihood of failure, whether in business or at a personal or professional level.

What should be in a business plan?

A business plan should commence with a **vision, mission and values statement**[21]. It should set goals, realistic objectives and attainable targets. These targets should also be stretch targets to challenge management[22] and include strategies as well as a plan of action. *A business plan is not static.* It must be a dynamic living document, providing a mechanism to resolve problems and maintain profitable growth.

What are the benefits of having a dynamic business plan?

Change is inevitable. A dynamic business plan can provide a framework to manage internal change and to meet the challenges and opportunities of external change. The process of developing a business plan commences with a Strengths Weaknesses Opportunities Threats analysis (SWOT)[23]. The SWOT, if performed well, will identify the opportunities and threats to the business and its strengths and weaknesses. My clients tell me the best SWOT sessions should be conducted by an external professional facilitator, who

---

21   See Chapter 3: Planning, section 1: Framework, part 3: Business values – are they of value?

22   See Chapter 3: Planning, section 1: Framework, part 2: Vision

23   See Chapter 4: Processes, section 1: Essentials, part 5: SWOT analysis

does not necessarily have an intricate knowledge of the business or industry. They are less likely to have internal business agendas or conscious or unconscious biases. The best SWOTs are derived from a well-facilitated process.

How can a business plan fit into the annual running of the business?

In writing a business plan, some of the greatest value is derived from the time spent thinking about the business – understanding its background and the external and internal aspects of the business and industry. A SWOT is a good example of this process.

The next step is to write a business plan. There are many different models and templates that can be used to write a business plan, and the choice of model is a matter of personal and professional choice. In my experience, the best plans result from a team effort, which includes input from key managers and provides greater scope for involvement and commitment. Even as the business owner or CEO, you may not be the smartest person in the room[24].

The ongoing value of a dynamic business plan is in monitoring the plan. I use the model in Figure 3 which breaks down the plan into 90-day projects, 1-year goals and a 3-year vision and this is aligned with the annual budget.

---

24 See Chapter 3: Planning, section 3: Communication, part 2: Are you a smart manager?

3 Year Vision

- What will be happening 3 years from now?
- Use correct language - the present state
- What does the business look like?
- Revenue, customers, profits etc.

1 Year Goals

- Specific goals in year 1 to achieve 3 year vision
- Must be measurable - how much, by when, etc.
- 7 - 8 goals

Dynamic Business Plan

90 Day Projects

- Projects make goals happen
- What projects need to be completed to achieve 1 year goals?
- Name each project by the result you are after

Actions

- Look at project list
- What actions need to be taken?
- Break down projects into achieveable actions
- Start with the verb (action) work e.g. call, write, meet

Figure 3: Dynamic Business Plan

The business plan is presented in *manageable and achievable bites, like eating an elephant.* At monthly management meetings, 90-day projects are monitored to check progress towards the overall vision. Small projects build towards the 1-year goals, which in turn form part of the 3-year vision. The power of this approach is that those involved can measure the progress against the plan and are therefore more committed. At the same time, financial performance is checked against the annual budget[25]. If circumstances change, priorities can

25   See Chapter 6: Profits, section 1: Measures, part 4: Is an annual budget really all that important?

be easily adjusted. With our logistics business, our goal was to be recognised as the pre-eminent provider of floor-ready merchandise services for suppliers to major retailers. When the retailers established distribution centres in Asia, we were forced to change our strategy to provide full warehousing services to SMEs.

Remember: business planning, like life, is a journey, not a project.

Do you have a business plan for *one year or three years*?

Is it **dynamic** and do you regularly refer to it to ensure its relevance?

3.2.3 What is your plan?

Boer maak 'n plan…

In Afrikaans, the language spoken by Dutch immigrant descendants living in South Africa, 'boer maak 'n plan' means a **'farmer makes a plan'**.

The deprivations and harshness of farming in a foreign land brought resolve and the need to plan around or solve these problems. Having travelled recently in southern Africa, I came across a similar saying in Zimbabwe where people often spoke about **'making a plan'**.

What does the saying really mean?

Not as it appears literally. The 'hidden' meaning is that you have an alternative plan – **a plan B** when your first plan fails or is impossible to implement. In other words, you need to be *flexible* and *adaptable* to solve a problem.

How does this equate to managing a business?

As business owners or managers, we need to plan in the first instance. As the saying goes, **'if you fail to plan, you plan to fail'**.

However, having a rigid plan may not work if circumstances change. Here is an example.

In our third-party logistics business, we were having difficulty getting our trucks unloaded on time at a retailer's distribution centre, despite meeting their strict time slots. It was OK for the distribution centre to run late unloading your trucks, but if your trucks failed to arrive at the designated time slot then you were 'fined'. What made the situation even worse was that to make the early morning delivery time slots, trucks had to battle peak hour traffic to and from the distribution centre. This became an expensive experience. Instead of three hours, it was taking six hours to deliver and unload. It was further compounded by our fixed-price delivery charge.

We had many meetings with distribution centre management, and despite their assurances, the situation did not improve.

What would solve our problem and be a 'win' for the distribution centre? Our Plan B.

By making some observations and talking to the receiving team at the distribution centre, a plan emerged. All loads were unloaded by hand onto a conveyor, rather than on wooden pallets. The individual cartons were scanned as they travelled up the conveyor belt. The distribution centre had a prime mover that was used for moving trailers around the receiving area.

We asked the distribution centre management whether we could trial loading a 40' container instead of an ordinary tautliner semi-trailer. We would bring in the loaded container early in the morning, before peak hour, and leave it in the receiving area for the distribution centre prime mover to move it onto the unloading conveyor when it suited the receiving team. The empty container would then be picked up at the next early morning delivery. After a short trial, it was a proven win/win for both us and the distribution centre. Delivery time halved, there was a massive increase in margin for us and the distribution centre was able to utilise their receiving area far more efficiently.

The success of the trial enabled us to purchase two second-hand and obsolete semi-trailers for 10% of their replacement value and establish a unique closed loop-delivery system that was extremely profitable.

We solved the waiting time problem and the peak hour travel problem which had initially appeared to be unresolvable. *We significantly increased our profits by having a Plan B.*

Like the farmer facing the unpredictability of the harsh African environment…

Remember: in any situation, you should always have a Plan B.

3.2.4 The New Year - before you move forward take a look back

'We do not learn from experience, we learn from reflecting on experience.'[26]

John Dewey – philosopher, psychologist, and educational reformer

The traditional Christmas and New Year summer holiday period in Australia is when employees head off for holidays. It is a good time for *managers and business owners to reflect* on the previous year.

While it is normally considered a good time to plan for the year ahead, by setting goals and targets ready for the challenge of the new year, it is also a good time to **'look back'** and reflect on the previous year.

Is looking back bad?

No.

If you are not reviewing the previous 12 months, you often lose perspective on what has been achieved and what has not worked out as planned. Here are **three questions** you should ask yourself and your team in looking back over the previous year:

---

26   John Dewey, *How We Think*, Heath and Company, 1910

1. **WHAT did we do *well* last year and WHY?**

While it is important to recognise and celebrate wins, it is just as important to ask the questions:
- '*How* did we have these wins?'
- '*What* were the actions that we as a team took to get this great result?'

Note the reasons down, share these with the team and have a goal to continue this strategy.

2. **WHAT did we do *badly* this year and WHY?**

Sadly, many of us blame others and make excuses as to why things fail. It's time to put our egos aside[27] and be honest as to the causes of the failures.
- '*Where* did we fail?'
- '*Where* did we not strive hard enough?'
- '*Where* did we not act like a team?'
- '*When* was the customer not put ahead of ourselves?'
- '*What* happened and what did YOU do to contribute to that result?'

Make a note of the answers to the above questions and ensure that you do not do that again. After all, as managers we are accountable.

Alexander the Great used Asian elephants in warfare

---

27   See Chapter 5: Productivity, section 3: Consistency, part 3: Procrastination and egos cost businesses…

3. **WHAT goals did we set this time last year that we did *not achieve* and WHY?**

   There is a quote attributed to Albert Einstein that says, 'Insanity is doing the same thing repeatedly and expecting different results'[28]. Establishing the same goals and associated actions as last year will most likely give you the same result.

   - '*Why* did we set them?'
   - '*Why* didn't we achieve them?'
   - '*Did* these goals really matter?'
   - 'Is it *different* this time?'

   Discuss with your team as to whether the goals are *still a priority*, and if they should be the same goals again for this year.

Having answered these questions honestly and openly, you and your team are *ready to set goals and plans for the next calendar year.*

Does your team have the *skills, capabilities, work ethic* and *behavioural characteristics* to be a **'winning' team** for next year?

---

28   There is some conjecture as to whether Einstein was the original source.

3.2.5 New Year's resolutions for you and your business

'We adopted a strategy that required our being smart and not too smart at that, only a very few times. Indeed, we now settle for one good idea a year.'[29]

Warren Buffett – business magnate, investor and philanthropist.

The start of the calendar year is a time for reflection, recharging your batteries and planning for the year ahead.

Did you achieve your professional or business goals?

If not, why not?

Many of us make long lists of New Year's resolutions that are unfortunately never fulfilled. Maybe we had too many resolutions, or they were too difficult, or we were just plain lazy. One study found that less than 10% of New Year's resolutions are ever completed or considered successful.

However, as business owners or managers, we are *obliged do better* and are expected to do better.

For example, as a manager or business owner, you will probably have a couple of new year's resolutions about being more productive, or expanding or improving your business.

Are they the *right goals*?

Will they make a *REAL difference* and become *habits* and a *mindset* so that you succeed now, and for the next 365 days?

As Warren Buffet suggests in the quote above, making a few significant decisions will make a real difference. With New Year's resolutions, set the right resolutions, limit the number and use the

---

29   Warren Buffett, *Warren Buffett on Business: Principles from the Sage of Omaha*, Wiley & Sons, 2009

KISS principle: keep it simple, stupid. By doing this, your decisions are more likely to be effective and result in changing your habits.

Here are *three resolutions* you could consider for next year with *three aims* of being *positive and habit-forming, changing your mindset* and having a *positive impact* on you, your business and your team.

1. Ask More Questions

How often do you meet people and find they rarely ask questions?

Asking questions is not a sign of weakness. Questions are a tool to drastically improve your knowledge, resources, and even your network. *Put your ego aside and ask questions.* You will be surprised at what you will learn. I recently attended a training course and met some new professional consultants. By asking questions, I found some surprising links with people we knew and experiences they had that could be useful in the future.

Asking questions is one of the most valuable skills a manager can have, whether it's asking for advice, asking for feedback, or simply asking for help. It also demonstrates empathy and builds understanding. Great leaders do not have all the answers, however, they usually ask the right questions.

2. Work On My Business, Not Just In It

Most businesses start with a technician wanting to work for themselves because they have technical skills[30]. However, as the business grows, there is a tendency to work on the activities you know and enjoy doing. That is *working in the business, not on the business.*

To build a successful team or business, you need to learn how to create an entity that can exist without you by leading rather than doing. Simply working harder or working longer hours is unlikely to

---

30   See Chapter 2: People, section 1: Leadership, part 5: Are you an intelligent boss?

improve your business as significantly as required or desired. While you may know your business better than anyone else, and are the most efficient person in the business, the time you spend doing jobs that other people could be doing, is *time not spent* running and improving your business.

I learnt this the hard way in my former logistics business. I was spending too much time calculating the productivity of the different sections of the business by employee and customer = *working in the business*. It dawned on me that someone else could prepare the productivity reports for me. With the completed reports, I could then concentrate on the areas that needed action, and highlight and praise good performance = *working on the business*.

So, force yourself to look at your organisation objectively and determine what needs to occur so you can achieve your goals.

3. Do More Networking

Networking is one of the most valuable tools you can have in your manager's toolbox. Knowing the right person provides opportunities to grow your business, through new markets or products and finding yourself a mentor. Managers or business owners who surround themselves with diverse, dynamic, long-standing and large networks increase their likelihood of success.

I was able to successfully find a prospective buyer for our logistics business through a networking contact[31] that went back over 25 years. However, networking needs to be approached with the mindset of maintaining a relationship and helping others. You are likely to have contacts, skills and experience that can assist others and, in turn, they are more likely to help you. *Remember: people do not like being used.*

---

31   See Chapter 5: Productivity, section 1: History, part 5: Networking

You are far more likely to develop relationships when you are not selling or asking for something. Networks are support systems. You are then more likely to gain assistance through your network when you need it.

So, force yourself to make phone calls, catch up for a coffee or join an organisation such as a professional association or a service club. You will be surprised how rewarding it is.

Have you **started thinking** about your New Year's resolutions?

Will these New Year's resolutions meet the **KISS (Keep It Simple Stupid) principle**?

Will they be **habit-forming**, **change your mindset** and have a **positive impact** on your team or business?

Hannibal of Carthage attacked Rome using African forest elephants, that were once common in Morocco

3.2.6 A new beginning

'To say it is life changing is an understatement — it is a new life, not life changing.'

Tim Boyle – Australia's first kidney and lower intestine transplant recipient

This is a quote from colleague and friend Tim Boyle, who became Australia's first kidney and lower intestine transplant recipient in October 2015.

Over 12 years ago, Tim received the news that his lower intestine was no longer working and it was removed. Although he could eat, he could only process 10% of his intake as nutrition and he had to be fed via an intravenous drip. Later, his kidneys failed which meant that each week he spent up to 50 hours attached to medical machines[32].

Despite these setbacks, Tim remained optimistic for the future, was committed to his young family and continued to build his business. While he had time to catch up for coffee, produce a monthly newsletter and *write a book,* we noticed a slow decline in his health and in the last few months, this became a rapid decline. Although he acknowledged this decline, we 'outsiders' feared for his future.

Tim's journey and his quote got me thinking: **How does this relate to business?**

Many businesses are like Tim's health. *Slow decline not noticed* by those in the business, whether it be the owners or employees, but noticed by those outside. **Complacency** and accepting the current situation in business can be **fatal**. This can happen without you realising the true situation and can result in business failure.

---

32 https://www.dailymail.co.uk/news/article-3323623/Father-spent-50-000-hours-hooked-intravenous-drip-Australian-small-bowel-kidney-transplant-vows-daughter-dinner.html

This is sometimes called the 'boiling frog syndrome' (BFS) and is based on the fable that if a frog is placed in boiling water it will jump out. However, if it is placed in water that is gradually heated then the frog will willingly be boiled alive. It is then too late for the frog and the consequences are explained in Charles Handy's *The Age of Unreason*.

Time for a new beginning...

So, what should you be doing?

What you should *not* be doing is relaxing and allowing the status quo to continue. It could be fatal to your business.

Here are some suggestions to get you thinking and acting:

1. **Learn lessons from last year**: Write down what you have learned – good and bad – and act on them for the next year
2. **Set goals for the next 12 months**: Write them down, be positive and ensure they are realistic and will make you look back in 12 months with a sense of achievement
3. **What bad habits should you eliminate?** We all have bad habits that if we change will make us, our staff and our customers more productive, engaged and motivated
4. **Thank your staff and customers**: In particular, those who helped you and the business in the past year. Hopefully, you would have done this before Christmas
5. **Clean up anything left over from the previous year**: There is nothing better than starting the new year with a 'clean slate'. Leftover tasks stop you moving forward with energy and enthusiasm for the new year deserves.

Think of Tim and remember: this year is an opportunity for **'a new life'**...

Postnote: If you haven't done so, why not consider becoming an organ donor?

It is easy to do. Unfortunately, most people don't, only because they haven't thought about it. Tim waited for four years and was unlikely to live to see Easter 2016.

3.2.7 Is success a matter of luck?

'Luck is where preparation meets opportunity.'[33]

Jack Gibson – legendary National Rugby League (NRL) coach

Too often these days, we hear that success is due to luck. Whether in the 'old' media or social media, we hear the same storyline – *success is a matter of luck.*

Is this really the case?

Perhaps all we need to do is visit Zimbabwe and get an appointment with Dr Mulongo (see Figure 4), a witch doctor or *In'yanga*. Referring to number 9 on the list, 'removal of bad lucky', we could simply ask Dr Mulongo to remove the spell using witchcraft.

As a dare while on a visit to Bulawayo several years ago, I visited Dr Mulongo and asked her whether she could assist the Wallabies, the Australian rugby union team, to win more matches by casting a spell on their opposition. Sadly, since this visit, their performance has deteriorated, especially against the All Blacks, their New Zealand rivals.

Contrast this approach with the late Jack Gibson, a legendary National Rugby League (NRL) coach in Australia from the late 1960s to the mid-1980s. He was known for his economy of words, and his notable and laconic quotes showed great wisdom and are still referred to today.

---

33   Andrew Webster, *Supercoach: The Life and Times of Jack Gibson*, Allen & Unwin, 2011

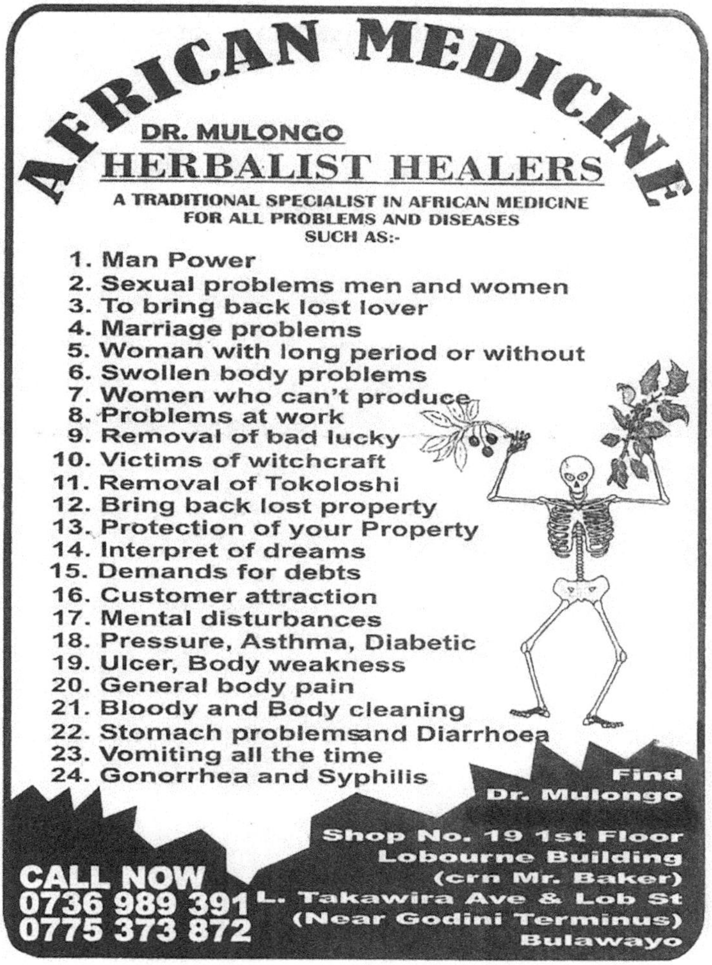

Figure 4: Removal of bad lucky

Gibson was totally unafraid of relegating to the bench any 'big name' players who did not perform. As the first coach to use computers to evaluate player performance, he *introduced new innovations* into the NRL from other sports, including American football and basketball. He was a great proponent of *careful planning* and *high levels of fitness,* and he effectively changed the game so it became more professional. This led to five consecutive premierships across two clubs.

During my period of over 20 years in business, there were many times when people considered that luck had made the business successful. However, I do not believe in luck creating success. Like Jack Gibson, I believe that *luck is where preparation meets opportunity*. You **make your own luck** through sound leadership, preparation and hard work.

In the early years, we were reliant on one of Australia's largest retailers for over 80% of our business. We worked hard to build a close working relationship with them, focusing on them as a customer and exceeding their expectations. When they changed their distribution model, introduced electronic commerce and forced suppliers to prepare their merchandise 'store ready' – picked and packed with an electronic invoice for each store – we were ideally positioned to take **advantage** of this opportunity.

We worked with the retailer, converting their suppliers into our customers. Once converted, we worked hard at being **'customer responsive'** and provided high level **'hands-on'** customer service. The business did not look back and many of these customers remained with the business until it was sold over 15 years later.

What are **three lessons from this story**?

1. *You make your own luck.*
   This is done by being prepared, understanding both your customer's needs and the requirements and changes in the market place. If you are prepared, you are in a prime position to take advantages of any opportunities that may arise.

   In this example, we were able to take advantage of the change in retailer-supplier relations.
2. *There is no substitute for hard work.*
   As I tell my children, the only place where reward comes before work is in the dictionary. Success comes from

preparation, working hard, learning from your mistakes and never giving up[34].

In this example, when 80% of our business was leaving due to the change in the supplier relationship, our hard work with the retailer gave us the opportunity to work with them and convert their suppliers to become our customers.

3. *Focus on the customer.*
Customers are the **lifeblood of any business**. Without them, you have no business. Focus on their needs, engage with them, meet them regularly, continually seek out their requirements and constantly remind them that you are looking after their interests.

By focusing on the major retailer, who was our customer, we developed a constructive working relationship where they were able to recommend our services to their suppliers.

As a business owner or manager, is your style to believe in Dr Mulongo's witchcraft to '**remove bad lucky**' or is your style more like the legendary coach Jack Gibson, where **careful planning and hard work leads to success**?

The elephants' closest living relative is the rock hyrax or dassie – a small furry mammal

---

34   See Chapter 4: Processes, section 2: Methods, part 6: Never, never, never give in

3.2.8 Business continuity - do you have a plan?

'Continuity does not rule out fresh approaches to fresh situations'[35]
Dean Rusk – US Secretary of State

What would happen if you did not turn up to work today?

This is a very important question for business owners.

Would your business continue to operate?

Would it continue to grow, and can you sell it?

Tim Boyle's[36] situation with his illness and ground-breaking medical operation is a good example of having a business continuity plan. As a finance broker, he was passionate about providing people with opportunities to own their own home. This was a good example of the 'why' of being in business, as described by Simon Sinek in *Start With Why*. Tim was not focused on what the business does but why it does it – to provide home owning opportunities.

Over the long years waiting for a suitable donor, while spending many hours on dialysis machines, Tim continued to build his business and *put in place contingencies for the business to operate without him.* While recovering in hospital, he talked to staff in the hospital at all levels, explaining how important it is own your own home. I witnessed nurses coming up to him and thanking him for giving them hope.

However, the real message was that his business continued to operate while he was busy 'not being there'. His staff of two continued to work without him.

Why?

Because there was a *business continuity plan* – it could operate without Tim being present.

---

35   Attributed to Dean Rusk, US Secretary of State 1961-1969
36   See Chapter 3: Planning, section 2: Roadmap, part 6: A new beginning

This is one of the biggest issues for SME owners – *the elephant in the room.*

Would your *business survive without you coming into work?*

If your *business cannot operate without you,* then your *business is vulnerable.* Should you wish to sell your business in the future, and the business is dependent on you daily, then what impact will this have on the value to a potential buyer?

The answer is obvious.

It is important to be a **'leader'** rather than a **'doer'** in your business, otherwise your business cannot operate or grow without you.

Putting it bluntly, the first step is to *put your ego aside* and plan to have your business operate without you. You can then go on holidays, be absent, protect your wealth, your family relationships and your health.

You have nothing to lose and everything to gain…

An elephant's brain is three to four times the size of a human's

3.3
COMMUNICATION

3.3.1 Don't judge a person until you have walked a mile in his shoes...

'You never really know a man until you understand things from his point of view, until you climb into his skin and walk around in it.'
Harper Lee – author of 'To Kill a Mockingbird'

This quote is a derivation of an old Cherokee proverb which states, *'Don't judge a man until you have walked a mile in his shoes.'*

What does this proverb mean to managers?

Have you ever worked for a manager that tells you to do something but does not understand the situation, because they have 'never been there or done that' before, and this annoys you?

As managers of people, we must be careful not to fall into this trap. Our staff will think we lack empathy and are incompetent or a poor manager. Certainly, in recent times, many politicians on both sides of the political divide in Australia have entered politics as political advisers, staffers and trade union officials – and have never run a business or worked in the private sector. Other examples are business consultants advising on a course of action even though they have never owned or managed a business or had their own money on the line.

This situation was illustrated recently when I took an elderly friend who uses a walking frame to our local multi-level shopping centre. He was unable to use the stairs and required an elevator.

We found out that the elevators were at opposite ends of the shopping centre. This meant walking further than more able-bodied people. I would never have realised this issue existed if I had not experienced it for myself. I now realise why he was reluctant to visit this shopping centre.

As this example shows, *you should try and understand someone before criticising them or making them do something that is unreasonable or very difficult* – unless you understand their experiences and challenges.

Can you remember the last time you did this?

As managers, we are all guilty of this at times. The challenge is to limit this behaviour as much as possible.

3.3.2 Are you a smart manager?

'If you are the smartest person in the room then you're in the wrong room.'
Anonymous

Michael Dell, founder of Dell Computers, has a similar quote: 'Try never to be the smartest person in the room. And if you are, I suggest you invite smarter people…or find a different room.'[37]

As managers, what does this mean?

Logically, the smartest person in the room should be the manager. After all, who will provide the direction and manage the organisation?

Quite clearly, this is wrong.

Why?

The people who think they are the smartest person in the room tend to have the last say and rarely listen to or acknowledge different ideas

---

37   https://www.graduationwisdom.com/speeches/0048-dell.htm

or opinions. Many show their disdain or disinterest by interrupting others in mid-sentence or displaying negative nonverbal traits such as rolling their eyes, looking away or checking their phone. I help organise an annual leadership training program for local businesses and organisations through our Rotary Club. Several years ago, a local council put up several candidates and one candidate refused to attend, stating, 'I have an MBA, so I don't need leadership training.'

It would have been a waste of time and money for them to attend, not because of their MBA, but because of their attitude.

However, *learning should continue throughout your life*, at work and outside work. Learning **does not stop** with finishing school or a degree[38]. *People only learn and grow when being challenged.* Being the smartest person in the room often means that you will not be challenged. Great managers surround themselves with people who challenge them as they realise that to continue to be relevant and innovative, you must be open to new ideas and concepts. By valuing other's opinions and accepting that you are not always the smartest person in the room, healthy, constructive and sometimes heated debates will help your organisation and help you.

A business owner I know, who is intelligent and well qualified academically, has failed to grow his business as profitably and as quickly as planned. While he is pleasant, polite and obviously intelligent, he is rarely challenged and appears to not listen to others. He also claims he has little time or interest to **read books**. It has adversely affected his staff turnover and business, as staff initiatives and ideas appear to be stifled. Being in charge does not mean you have all the answers. I have found that some of the smartest people can be found anywhere in an organisation, you just **need to find and develop them.**

---

38   See Chapter 3: Planning, section 3: Communication, part 6: Reading is not just for Christmas…

While working for a transport business many years ago, I found a driver who had the attributes and energy to become a qualified driver-trainer. Despite initially being hostile to management, he turned his experience into a new position and he greatly added to the business by training drivers, thereby reducing accidents, injuries, and fuel consumption. Furthermore, and probably more importantly, this improved his motivation and morale, as well as his own self-image.

As managers, we probably all have the tendency to act like the smartest person in the room.

The challenge is to *resist this temptation*, without, of course, abdicating your responsibility as a manager.

Here are **three suggested** approaches:

1. *Ask more questions and listen to the answers.* Questions are powerful leadership tools[39]. Resist telling people what to do and respond to ideas with questions which help you and others better develop their ideas. Seek first to understand before offering your own perspective.
2. *Have the courage to remain silent* and help others decide. This does not mean that you cannot veto an idea or approach. Through open questioning techniques, ideas can be modified or adapted in a constructive way to get the best outcome.
3. *View ideas as a 'glass half full'* not *'half empty'*, as it is a positive approach. People respond to the positive rather than the negative. **Negative discussions should only centre around risks.**

---

39   See Chapter 4: Processes, section 1: Essentials, part 4: Questions and answers

These approaches often challenge us as managers. However, it is highly likely to *engage* and *motivate* our subordinates, make them feel *part of a team* and allow *new ideas and approaches* to surface. You will be challenged.

As a manager, can you resist the temptation and follow these approaches?

In *Sam Walton: Made in America,* Sam Walton, the founder of Walmart, identified an open-door policy of encouragement, which allowed good ideas to surface, as one of the strategies that made Walmart a success.

Why don't you **'give it a go'?**

3.3.3 Using visual symbols to communicate...

'The best leaders… almost without exception and at every level, are master users of stories and symbols.'[40]

Tom Peters – business author

We often hear business leaders and politicians trying to communicate messages unsuccessfully.

Why?

Are they using too many words, the wrong words, or just words?

Communication is not just verbal. It is estimated that 65% to 90% of all communication is nonverbal. Eye contact, facial expressions, appearance and gestures influence how you interpret the message.

This is where the use of symbols is important in communicating. This can be used in the workplace.

Recently, I was confronted with trying to express the importance and urgency of cultural change to an organisation that was underperforming. Presenting to the board, I realised that the use of symbols

---

40 Attributed to Tom Peters, US writer on business management practices

or visual imagery would help communicate the issues and how to manage the change.

The visual imagery I decided to use was taken directly out of Jim Collins' *From Good to Great – Why Some Companies Make the Leap and Others Don't*. I used the symbol of a *bus*. The symbolism was very easy to understand.

Following the presentation, I then further developed the concept by using a model of a toy bus. The bus had the company's logos on the side, and on the roof was an arrow pointing forwards – indicating progress and moving ahead – along with the Jim Collins quote:

'Get the right people on the bus, the wrong people off the bus, and the right people in the right seats.'

Later, the toy bus sat on the meeting room table for all to see and we added Lego people getting on and off the bus. Normal people getting on and pirates, wizards and clowns getting off the bus. The toy bus was regularly referred to when explaining a person's performance or suitability and became a *clear way of communicating*.

Staff were often asked: **'Are you on the bus?'** and **'Are they on the bus?'**

It became a powerful visual symbol. When management spoke about what needed to happen, it was described in terms of being on the bus. It was a clear message and was understood by everyone from the managing director to the staff on the shop floor.

We implemented daily 'toolbox' meetings with staff and called the meeting location 'the bus stop', further reinforcing the message.

Using symbols in business as a tool is a very important part of communicating, both with your current and prospective customers and staff. *If the symbol is compelling enough, it will become part of the organisation's culture.*

Can you think of a symbol used by an organisation that is easily recognisable and understood?

What **visual symbols** could you use to communicate more effectively?

3.3.4 Business storytelling

'Storytelling is about two things; it's about character and plot.'[41]
George Lucas – American filmmaker

What has a quote from a famous movie director got to do with business storytelling?

Using stories in business as a communication tool is a very important part of communicating with staff and both current and prospective customers. *If the story is compelling enough or inspiring enough, it will become part of the culture of the business and demonstrate your company's values and history.* More importantly, it helps sell your products and services.

Everybody likes a good story and, as George Lucas says, the plot and character are vital. I find stories about how businesses start compelling and fascinating. Hewlett-Packard was started in a garage by Dave Packard and Bill Hewlett in 1938. The garage is now part of company culture and a photograph of the famous garage is displayed in all HP offices. *What an inspiring story.*

I worked for a company where the owner lost the business his father and uncle had established after fleeing the Nazis in Europe. He and his daughter then started a new business in their rented flat, working from their kitchen table. It later became the largest supplier of sleeping bags in Australia.

What a **compelling story for staff and customers...**

---

41   https://www.theverge.com/2013/6/13/4427444/
       lucas-spielberg-storytelling-in-games-its-not-going-to-be-shakespeare-usc

People, whether staff or customers, warm to stories of success from hardship – a plot and character, just as George Lucas suggests. It's emotional and uplifting. However, the story must be authentic. If you are not authentic, it damages you and your business or brand.

When consulting to a locally-owned travel business in Nepal, how the owner started the business was an inspiring story. As a young boy, the owner had watched groups trekking through his village in northern Nepal. He had a vision and decided to create his own future. While in his early teens, he went to Kathmandu to attend high school, without his family. In Nepal, high schools are only in the largest cities. From there, he worked in a hotel as a porter before moving into reception. To gain practical experience in trekking, he became a guide and then completed his university studies before establishing his own tour company. All this was less than 20 years ago. This business is now one of the largest trekking companies in Nepal. As well as offering employment and training in a comparatively poor country, he also has *a mission to give back something to the people of Nepal.* He instigated school building projects in poor and remote areas, as well as making significant financial donations to schools in these areas.

Both are good examples of stories that can **inspire staff** because they explain where they came from, help embody the values and provide the foundation of the culture and vision for the company.

Do you have some great stories you can tell your customers and staff?

Will it help add **colour** to your communication?

3.3.5 Never never say these things...

*'Don't go around saying the world owes you a living.
The world owes you nothing. It was here first.'*[42]

Mark Twain – American writer and humourist

Too often, when service providers, managers and staff fail to manage in a proactive way and things fail or do not go the way they expected, they come up with excuses.

What are the differences between reasons and excuses?

The measurement of success in business today is **performance**. Whether you are an honest and pleasant person, or related to the boss or not, is irrelevant if you are not contributing to the business's performance in a positive way. Too often, we hear about employees being unfairly treated when a business folds or lays off staff. However, perhaps rather than blaming 'someone else' – whether it is the owner, managers, the market or customers – the employees could have taken effective action that may have prevented the current situation.

I call this **'discretionary effort'**: the difference in the level of effort one is capable of bringing to an activity or a task, and the effort required to get by or make do. In other words, *'going the extra mile'*...

Here is a list of phrases to avoid, which are **excuses** and not reasons:

1. **'They didn't get back to me'** – so you did not follow up?
2. **'I thought someone else was taking care of it'** – so you don't take responsibility in your job'?
3. **'No one ever told me'** – so you don't communicate with those around you?

---

42   Attributed to Samuel Clemens, pen name Mark Twain, American writer, humourist, entrepreneur and publisher

4. **'I didn't have time'** – did you have time to talk around the water cooler or photocopier?
5. **'I didn't think to ask about that'** – so you don't think about your job?

If there are roadblocks in the business, whose job is it to remove them?

Yours or someone else's?

Sometimes, in business, there are too many people talking about their rights, what they think they are entitled to, rather than their responsibilities for taking initiative and being proactive[43].

Good business owners and managers love employees who *remove roadblocks* and are positive and proactive.

My observation from over 30 years in business is that if you use excuses like those above, then you are the roadblock.

Everybody learns from experience and learning is a 'state of mind'…

Where can you display positive discretionary effort?

Can you make that extra phone call to the customer or provide wise counsel to a junior employee?

Elephants' intestines can be up to 19 metres in length

---

43   See Chapter 4: Processes, section 3: Lessons, part 1: Above and below the line thinking

3.3.6 Reading is not just for Christmas...

'Not all readers are leaders, but all leaders are readers.'[44]

Harry S. Truman – former US President

Several years ago, I was assisting with managing a three-day residential leadership program called 'The Challenge to Lead' for our local Rotary Club. The program was run by professional facilitators who had donated their time to conduct the program. One of the facilitators asked the question:

'Who here has read a management or leadership book in the last 12 months?'

Of the 28 people in the room, only two put up their hands. I was horrified. I personally try to read a book a month on leadership and management, whether they are biographies of famous people or management books, in addition to novels and books on history.

The facilitator's comment was, 'Readers are leaders'

It was interesting that people attending a leadership course had not seen the need to increase their knowledge and seek out new ideas by reading. Billionaire investor Warren Buffett reads 500 pages a day, Bill Gates reads 50 books per year and Mark Zuckerberg reads two books per month.

However, successful people do not just read anything. They are selective, preferring to be educated rather than entertained.

Why is reading books, particularly management and leadership books important?

- We can learn from the experience of smart people –
  Management by Peter Drucker

---

44 https://www.truman.edu/about/history/our-namesake/truman-quotes/

- It opens up your mind to new ideas – *Good to Great* by Jim Collins
- It can be inspirational, particularly biographies – *Not for Turning. The Life of Margaret Thatcher* by Robin Harris
- It shows you how to do things – *The One Minute Manager* by Ken Blanchard and Spencer Johnson
- It stimulates the mind and gets you thinking – *How to Win Friends and Influence People* by Dale Carnegie
- It provides a framework for leadership – *The Seven Habits of Highly Effective People* by Stephen R. Covey.

Furthermore, reading elevates you above the **daily grind of work,** and can inspire you and give you **new ideas.** Reading is a form of learning and can **stimulate your thinking processes**, providing ideas from a **different viewpoint.**

If you do not have time for reading then another alternative is listening to audiobooks. I listen to audiobooks or podcasts while driving. Instead of listening to trivial talkback radio shows, I use the time to *increase my knowledge.*

With some planning, reading can become a **lifetime habit** and make you a **better leader and manager.**

Reading is not just for Christmas; however, it is a good time to begin.

What books should you read?

Make a list of books that would be of benefit to you as a manager.

Should you set a time-bound goal to read books on your reading list?

3.3.7 Christmas…it's that time of year again

*'The thing about Christmas is that it almost doesn't matter
what mood you're in or what kind of year you've had –
it's a fresh start.'* [45]

Kelly Clarkson – American songwriter and philanthropist

As business owners and managers, the Christmas period can be a period of joy and celebration or a disaster.

Every year, we hear stories of work Christmas parties that go wrong – drunkenness, inappropriate and embarrassing behaviour, work accidents and the like. Often, management or the organisation is blamed for the outcomes. It's even more disappointing when it is traditionally a **period of cheer and goodwill**. In Australia, it is also the start of the summer holiday period so generally everybody is in good spirits.

The Christmas party provides a *great opportunity* to build on the season of goodwill and *to say thank you*. Any manager who does not take this opportunity has failed as both a leader and a manager.

I can remember a Christmas party where the staff looked forward to the event and brought their families, including children and grandchildren, to enjoy the jumping castle, rides, ice cream and soft drinks. The free raffles were fun until the business owner's numbered ticket was picked from the barrel. He promptly walked up and collected his prize. His managers were horrified and embarrassed because it displayed a *lack of self-awareness and leadership*. They also witnessed the negative reaction from the staff and their families. A better option would have been to say, 'Draw the raffle again' and put your staff and families first, demonstrating you are a leader.

---

45   Attributed to Kelly Clarkson, American singer-songwriter

Another example was related to me by a friend. At their staff Christmas party, the CEO came down from the top floor, had her meal and chatted briefly to her general managers before disappearing back to her office. All without thanking the staff for their efforts during the year or wishing them all the best for the festive season. This was left to her deputy. This **total lack of leadership** was noted by the staff attending. **If you do not show your staff respect it will not be reciprocated.** A quiet and sincere speech of less than a minute would have created a different outcome.

So, what should you, as a manager, do for your staff at Christmas?

Celebrations aside, the traditional period of goodwill is an excellent opportunity as a manager to *'rise to the occasion'* and *display leadership*[46]. Talk to all your staff and their families. Display graciousness and sincerity about your staff's efforts. Wish them the best and paint hope and opportunity for the future. It is a **time for renewal and evaluation,** so take advantage of this great opportunity...

Elephants produce up to 1 tonne of manure per week

---

46   See Chapter 2: People, section 1: Leadership

4
PROCESSES

F ollowing planning, the next step or third 'P' in the five dimensions of improving business performance is processes. What method of cooking are we going to use to eat the elephant? Do we know what tools, equipment and processes are required by the team to successfully cook the elephant? We need shovels to dig the pit, rocks to lay inside the pit and knives to skin the elephant. How many people are needed? If we choose to cook the elephant in a pot, how can we fit it in? Cutting up the elephant into small pieces will require a large team of people. Barbecuing the elephant will also require cutting it into small pieces.

No matter what method of cooking is selected, we must firstly compare each process. What essential equipment is needed for each of the cooking methods? What is the most cost-effective way to cook the elephant? What do we need to know to do the job? Are there lessons from past experiences of cooking an elephant that tell us what the best processes are? Have we researched the best methods?

Elephants can't jump

4.1
ESSENTIALS

4.1.1 Problems

'Insanity: doing the same thing over and over again and expecting different results.'[1]

Albert Einstein – scientist

Many of us in business are confronted with problems – whether it is the business failing, parts of the business not performing or relationships at work deteriorating. I suspect that you have agonised about problems like these. The reasons are likely to be complex and there are probably no simple solutions.

However, *the first step is to admit there is a problem.* I have seen many leaders in business refusing to admit they have a problem, even though it is obvious to everybody around them, and often to themselves, although they refuse to confront it. This could be due to ego, ignorance, incompetence or an unwillingness to face reality. It is highly unlikely to go away and is probably only going to get worse and become more complicated as staff and customers begin questioning your judgement and leadership. Admitting that you have a problem to yourself, your family and your staff is essential.

---

[1] Although this is attributed to Albert Einstein there is no substantive evidence that he is originator of this quote

The second step is critical. This is where you either turn things around or continue failing to resolve the problem. The failing business person tries to justify the failure – 'it's the market', 'it's the internet', and so on.

As a manager or business owner, it is only a problem or a failure if it continues. Like the Albert Einstein quote on insanity, we must change something to get the desired result. The status quo is not an option. Do not identify an external reason for the problem as this is a 'cop out'. You are disowning the problem – 'it's the economy', 'it's the high exchange rate', 'it's poor staff'.

The key to success is to take a few steps that will not allow you to justify the problem. The first step is to act, even if it is just one small step. Using personal fitness as an example, the hardest step in improving your fitness is putting on your gym gear. By taking the first step, you are on the way to solving the problem of improving your fitness. Momentum has now commenced, and this will help solve other problems, both now and in the future.

As former American president Franklin D. Roosevelt said, 'a smooth sea never made a skilled sailor'[2]

There is no shame in recognising a problem or failure, providing you do something about it. *Learning from mistakes is only common sense and allows you to grow.*

That's what good leaders do.

Elephants use their trunks as snorkels when swimming

---

2   Attributed to US President Franklin D. Roosevelt

4.1.2 Priorities...

'Having my priorities in order has really helped me look better, fresher and more relaxed.'[3]

Kim Cattrall – Canadian actress formerly in Sex and the City

Maybe a quote from a TV star is not what you would expect for a chapter about priorities in work and business. However, it does highlight the fact that, if you have your priorities in order, you can achieve great things and not be sidetracked by unimportant issues.

Let me give you an example. When my daughter popped in after work one day, I asked casually how things were going in her job with a multi-national company. She started to complain that the new managing director had decreed that only white coffee cups were to be used. She wanted to use her *Lord of the Rings* coffee cup. Other people were also complaining.

So, what would be your advice for my daughter? Be defiant and show independence and continue to use her *Lord of the Rings* cup? It's all about priorities. Is it important? Possibly demotivating, irritating and annoying? 'Yes'. But important? 'No'.

Unfortunately, these types of decrees are not uncommon. Marius Kloppers, the former managing director of BHP Billiton, sent out an edict about desk 'etiquette' that bordered on the neurotic at a time when the company had both great opportunities and, of course, many problems. He subsequently left the company with very little to show for his tenure at the helm except many missed opportunities.

Micromanagement is normally a red flag that may indicate that management does not know how to prioritise, treat staff as not

---

3   Interview with Kim Cattrall on 30 May 2008 (https://www.goodhousekeeping.com/ life/inspirational-stories/interviews/a12493/kim-cattrall-interview/)

important and are not up to the 'real' job. I once worked for a manager who was obsessed with orderliness. All prospective customers
were placed in labelled manila folders and filed (and that's where
they stayed) while he complained that I should not keep active files
on the floor near my desk as it made my office untidy. Perhaps it did
make my office untidy. It certainly did not stop my success in achieving sales. Another good example from years ago was when I was
studying and working full-time. I thought it would be a good idea to
give my then manager a draft of one of my assignments related to our
industry. He proceeded to mark the spelling and check the grammar.
This was before spellcheck.

...Little wonder he was dismissed some years later.

A very relevant quote from Heiner Karst's *Life Learnings of a Life
Coach* clearly explains the situation with the metaphor: 'Do you think
a dog in the hunt has time to scratch for fleas?'.

Have you got your priorities right?

Are you concentrating on the **fleas** rather than the **bigger picture**?

By *concentrating on the right priorities*, life and work are far less
complicated. You are more likely to be much happier and more
successful.

An elephant's trunk has 100,000
different muscles

4.1.3 The 5 Whys

'For want of a nail, a shoe was lost,
for want of a shoe, a horse was lost,
for want of a horse, a rider was lost,
for want of a rider, an army was lost,
for want of an army, a battle was lost,
for want of a battle, the war was lost,
for want of the war, the kingdom was lost,
and all for the want of a little horseshoe nail.'

From Confesio Amantis, a 14th century poem by John Gower

Have you heard of the 5 Whys?

The 5 Whys is an analysis method used by Toyota Motor Corporation to find the root cause of a problem, not the symptom. It digs beneath the outward symptoms to find the REAL cause. The premise is that systems fail, not people. It is a very powerful management tool.

The method involves asking 'Why …?' five times in succession.

This may sound simplistic. However, it requires thought and intelligent application to ask the right 'Why'.

As the questioner, you may need discipline and persistence to follow the methodology. The answer to one question leads you into framing the next 'Why'.

It may not be possible to ask or answer the next question immediately, as you may need to collect and analyse additional information to ensure the question is answered properly. This may also require brainstorming.

This methodology requires practice, and the more you use and apply it, the more you'll begin to find the real underlying root causes of problems. By the time you get to the fourth or fifth 'Why', you are very likely to be looking at *management practices rather than just symptoms.*

Here is a simple example.

Five Whys Problem Solving	
Problem: The car won't start	**Reason**
1. Why?	The battery is flat.
2. Why is the battery flat?	The alternator is not working.
3. Why is the alternator not working?	The alternator belt is broken.
4. Why is the alternator belt broken?	The alternator belt was well past its useful life and had not been replaced.
5. Why is that?	The vehicle was not maintained in accordance with a maintenance schedule. There is no efffective maintenance system in place.

Figure 5: Five Whys of Problem Solving

A true-life example of management system failure was the 1986 Space Shuttle Challenger tragedy. Millions of people watched in horror as it exploded shortly after launch on live TV. It was caused by faulty 'O' rings and was a systemic failure of management systems in the space program.

When solving a problem using the 5 Whys, a *common error is to stop too soon*. People keep taking the first or second simple answer, blinded by the symptoms or settling for the first 'apparent' cause.

Don't accept 'it's just human error' or 'they made a mistake'. Mistakes happen. This is why robust quality systems are needed. Systems must be designed with built-in controls that help prevent the problem occurring in the first place, detect it if it does occur and then do something effective to stop it recurring.

Remember: you are looking for the root cause. Simple answers are most likely to be symptoms, as they are the outward signs of a problem that has been observed. They are unlikely to be the real root cause. Good quality management systems insist on a systematic approach to dealing with nonconformity, involving corrective and preventive actions. This can lead to massive improvements in an organisation's performance.

The example of the flat battery illustrates how a system of maintenance would have prevented the problem occurring. Money would have been saved on repairs, time would not have been lost while having the vehicle repaired, staff and customers would not have been delayed while waiting for the vehicle, and so on.

Can you think of a problem in your business or workplace where you could uncover the root cause using the 5 Whys?

4.1.4 Questions and answers

'Judge a man by his questions rather than by his answers.'[4]
Voltaire – French philosopher

One of the biggest mistakes we can make as managers is to **talk too much** and **ask too few enough questions**.

Are you a manager who suffers from *'I' strain* – I did this, I do this, I, I, I…?

Furthermore, if we do ask questions, do we **listen to the answer**?

Asking questions is one of the most effective ways of **gaining information and eliciting team cooperation**. It is therefore one of the best tools available to managers.

The skill in asking questions is to know **what** type of question to ask, **when** to ask it and **how** to ask it.

---

4   Attributed to Francois-Marie Arouet better known as Voltaire, French philosopher

There are two main types of questions:

1. *Closed questions* – these are those questions that require a one-word answer, normally 'yes' or 'no'. They should be avoided unless you are clarifying a position or answer.
2. *Open questions* – these are questions that elicit an open response where, if handled carefully, you can obtain valuable information and opinions, and have your staff committed to the organisation.

A useful technique in asking questions is to start the question with one of the following: **W**hy, **W**here, **W**hen, **W**ho, **W**hat, and **H**ow.

You can continue a conversation and explore ideas by rolling through the five Ws and Hs:

- 'Where' did it happen?
- 'When' did it happen?
- 'Who' was involved?
- 'What' happened?
- 'Why' did it happen?
- 'How' did it happen?

Other types of questions include:

1. *Direct questions* – can be used to slow down a fast talker, confront an obstructionist or draw out a reluctant participant.
2. *Leading questions* – should be generally avoided but can be used to gain support or bring a meeting to a close.

---

5   See Chapter 4: Processes, section 3: Lessons, part 5: Process improvement

3. *Ambiguous questions* – when more than one answer is possible and can also be used to provoke a response, slow down a domineering talker, start a discussion or spark some action.
4. *Provocative questions* – should be used with care and often used to provoke a response or defend a position
5. *Rhetorical questions* – very effective in putting an issue 'to bed' and moving on.
6. *Redirected questions* – used by politicians to avoid answering the question.

Also, questions are good tools to have when conducting a meeting. More importantly, we should avoid asking questions that:

1. Are closed questions (yes/no) unless you follow up with a direct or factual question.
2. Invoke antagonisms.
3. Are of a personal nature which may embarrass.
4. Are sarcastic.

So, now the question I ask is '**how active is your listening?**'
Are you getting the feedback you desire?
Does the person you are questioning feel that you are **interested** in and **actively listening** to their answers?

Elephant tusks never stop growing

4.1.5 SWOT analysis

'Proper planning and preparation prevents poor performance.'[6]
Stephen Keague – Irish author

The aim of this section is to explain the benefits of performing a SWOT analysis on your organisation. It is not how to perform a SWOT, which can be found on the internet and in management books, but *why SWOTs should be done* and who should conduct them to achieve the best outcome.

What is a SWOT analysis?

SWOT is an acronym that stands for **Strengths, Weaknesses, Opportunities, and Threats**. A SWOT analysis is an organised list of a business's greatest strengths, weaknesses, opportunities, and threats. It is a planning tool which businesses can use at any time to assess a changing environment and respond proactively.

Here are some important SWOT concepts:

- SWOT analysis is part of a business review.
- Strengths and weaknesses are generally *internal* to the business – for example, internal resources and capabilities such as peoples' skill levels, business processes and assets.
- Opportunities and threats tend to be *external* to the business – such as the economy, competitors, new technology and suppliers.
- Strengths and opportunities are *positive* to the business.
- Threats and weaknesses are normally *negative* to the business.

---

6   Stephen Keague, *The Little Red Handbook of Public Speaking and Presenting,* Createspace Independent Publishers, 2012

- The outcome of a SWOT analysis should result in a dynamic action plan, not a static statement.

The major problem with a SWOT is that too often it results in a list of statements for each of the four components. It is not an action plan. **This is the challenge for management.** Each of the four sections of the quadrant are linked to each other, so a list of actions can be created. These are shown below.

Internal

STRENGTHS Add value and offer a competitive advantage	**WEAKNESSES** Detract from value and put at competitive disadvantage
OPPORTUNITIES Opportunities in the market or environment which provide potential benefits	**THREATS** Threats beyond your control that pose risks to the organisation

Positive (left side) **Negative** (right side)

External

Figure 6: Four Quadrants of a SWOT

Here are the six questions that should be asked:

1. *Strengths – Weaknesses:* What actions can be implemented using the organisation's strengths to overcome the identified weaknesses?
2. *Opportunities – Threats:* What actions resulting from the identified opportunities can be used to overcome or reduce the threats?
3. *Strengths – Opportunities:* What are the actions that can leverage off your organisation's strengths and take advantage of the identified opportunities?
4. *Strengths – Threats:* Using the organisation's strengths, what actions can eliminate or reduce threats to your organisation?
5. *Opportunities – Weaknesses:* Considering the opportunities, what actions can be taken to overcome the organisation's weaknesses?
6. *Weaknesses – Threats:* What actions are required to overcome the organisation's weaknesses, to assist in preparing to face threats, both now and in the future?

The larger the tusks, the more attractive a male elephant is to a female elephant

In Figure 7 below, the plans of action are shown visually.

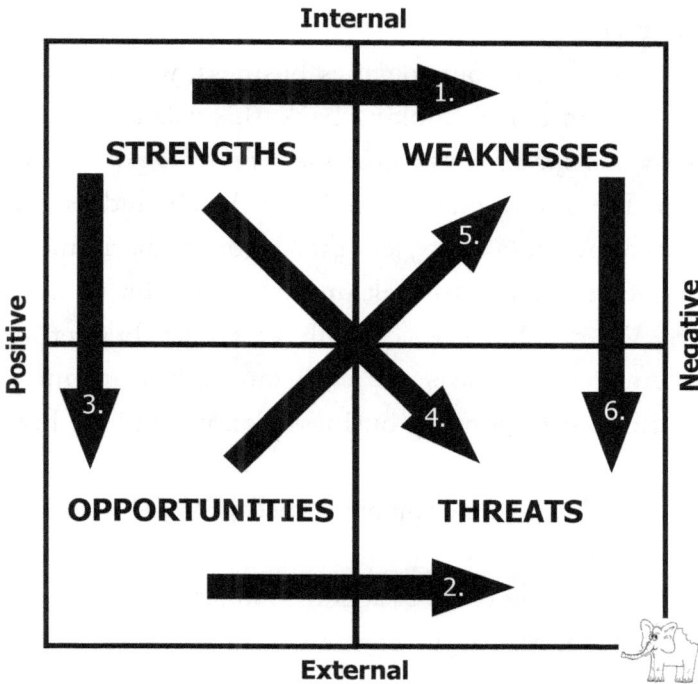

Figure 7: Action Plans from a SWOT

In answering these questions and forming the resulting actions, plans can be developed which can then become part of the strategic business plan. Performing a SWOT analysis is a vital part of creating a business plan and should be done every 12 months. *I recommend conducting a strategy review meeting at least once a year, beginning with a SWOT analysis.* In my experience, SWOT sessions should be performed with the management team, preferably with an independent facilitator. The independent facilitator is less likely to have a personal agenda and can impartially manage the discussions. When a new client first meets with me, we normally complete a SWOT session. This session may extend over two to three meetings depending on what is found. This establishes the groundwork for understanding the business and the foundations of a business plan.

In over 15 years in our logistics business, we only performed a SWOT session twice. Looking back, this was a major strategic error. *We missed out on opportunities and failed to act on some of our weaknesses.* There were many reasons for this, including the reluctance to face the brutal facts, less than rigorous discipline by some partners and reluctance to seek professional external advice and assistance. We did, however, compile an annual budget in which our performance was measured each month but, in hindsight, a SWOT with a corresponding business plan would have been more beneficial[7].

When was the last time you performed a SWOT analysis session with your team?

Were the resulting plans of action completed?

Did they form part of the business plan?

4.1.6 Measuring

'What gets measured gets done.'[8]

Peter Drucker – business writer and philosopher

This is a great quote for business or life, if you want to achieve your objectives or improve performance.

As the saying goes, 'If you can't measure it, you can't manage it.'[9]

In business, this means all areas from people and processes to

---

7   See Chapter 3: Planning, section 2: Road Map, part 2: Business plan – why is
     the journey more important than the destination?

8   Peter Drucker, *The Practice of Management,* Harper & Row, 1954

9   https://guavabox.com/if-you-cant-measure-it-you-cant-improve-it

performance. However, *in business it is important to identify the main 'things' that will ensure your business's success.* These are often called key performance indicators, or KPIs for those who wish to use three letter acronyms[10]. I shy away from using so-called management jargon and acronyms as it is often pretentious, arrogant, and only serves to complicate simple processes, ideas and concepts.

The identification of KPIs that drive the success of your business should **not exceed three to five measures or benchmarks**, otherwise it becomes too complicated and difficult to maintain.

KPIs need to be SMART:

- SPECIFIC – must be clear and concise so that everybody understands it
- MEASURABLE – must be based on performance or behaviour that can be measured objectively
- ACHIEVABLE – must be attainable and what is required
- REALISTIC – must be a goal that can be realistically achieved and should represent significant progress from the status quo
- TIMELY – must have a timeline to be achieved by (e.g. a certain date).

Using a transport business as an example, a KPI could be the number of kilometres travelled per vehicle per week to ensure an acceptable return on investment.

It could look something like this: by 30th June, the average kilometres travelled per week must be 8,000km per week. Currently, the average is 5,000km per week.

---

10   See Chapter 5: Productivity, section 2: Change, part 1: What is a KPI?

- SPECIFIC – 8,000km per week
- MEASURABLE – kilometres per week is measurable objectively on a weekly basis
- ACHIEVABLE – 8,000km per week is achievable if the truck works 2 shifts per day and/or 6 days per week
- REALISTIC – it is realistic and is greater than the status quo of 5,000km per week
- TIMELY – must be achieved by 30th June.

By implementing this KPI, performance can be measured on a weekly basis and compared week by week. The weekly KPI can then be used to implement a plan of action to achieve the required objectives.

In conclusion, by using SMART indicators your business objectives can be achieved providing you act on the KPIs to ensure you meet the required objectives. Otherwise with no objective measurement system in place and no management the status quo will remain and, more than likely, performance will deteriorate.

Can you determine the *key drivers of your business*?

Can they be easily measured?

By identifying and measuring these KPIs you can improve your business performance.

Elephants can be right or left 'tusked' (handed)

4.2
METHODS

4.2.1 Is running a business like a marriage?

'A successful marriage is an edifice that must be rebuilt every day.'[11]

Andre Maurois – French author

I have been married for over 30 years. I am truly blessed to have shared those years with my wonderful wife in a great marriage, with all its joys and challenges.

Can lessons can be learned from a great marriage that can be applied to managing a successful business?

Yes, there are many...

Here are just **three lessons** from a successful marriage that can be applied to business.

1. **Communication**

    Continuous two-way, frank and honest communication is the hallmark of a successful marriage. Problems can be aired and solved constructively, and the future discussed. It is the same in business. Communication with staff, between departments and with customers

---

11   Andre Maurois, *The Art of Living*, translated from the French by James Whitall, English University Press, 1940

provides the mechanics of a successful business. Goals and successes can be shared, and problems solved. Communication is about caring and sharing. Customers and staff do not want to be left 'in the dark'. **Two-way continuous communication** helps ensure staff and customers feel valued and are committed to you and the organisation. Too often, we become complacent and fail to communicate regularly.

Some years ago, in our logistics business, I increased the rates for a customer without communicating the reasons. They immediately sought competitive proposals and then advised us they wanted to leave. Luckily, our operations manager was able to remedy the situation by discussing the reasons for the increase, only to find that the order and customer profile had changed significantly and the rate schedule was now no longer suitable. Frank two-way communication had not occurred, we did not know the profile had changed and we had not advised the reasons for the increase. I learnt my lesson.

2. **Commitment**

Any relationship or partnership is not all smooth sailing, whether it is managing a business or a marriage. Many obstacles are outside our control but must still be faced. Reflecting on our marriage, we have had to face challenges along the way. Whether they were family issues or geographic isolation from family and friends, we were committed to making it a success. The same principles can be used for businesses.

If you are **committed** to managing a business effectively or growing a business, you need to meet the challenges as they emerge. Often, we face crises that could destroy the business. In our logistics business, there was a situation where a customer owed us over $350,000 and claimed they could not pay. If they failed to pay, our business would probably have been destroyed. Luckily, through commitment in enforcing a payment plan, we were able to get the money owed and save the business.

3. **Celebration**

Too often we do not celebrate what is important, whether in business or in a marriage. Celebrating marriage success such as anniversaries or milestones is important.

Business is no different. Looking back on our business, we rarely celebrated successes such as winning a new contract. Later, we found out that the staff wanted to know our success and suggested we should celebrate with a barbeque or luncheon. We did, however, recognise staff service and made a big deal about its importance. Our business had staff that had been with us from the beginning and were still there 15 years later. We **celebrated** this by presenting awards and a gift at our annual company conference.

As the quote from Andre Maurois suggests, success in marriage is about continuously rebuilding. The same goes for managing a successful business.

Communication, Commitment and **Celebration** is a good start. Complacency leads to stagnation and, often, failure. This is sometimes called the 'boiling frog syndrome', as mentioned earlier in this book[12].

What are your plans to *continually improve* your organisation or business?

---

12   See Chapter 3: Planning, section 2: Roadmap, part 6: A new beginning

Can you *communicate more in a positive way?*
Are *celebrating your successes* with your staff?

4.2.2 'Nothing is easy'

'Nothing is easy, but who wants nothing?'[13]

Donald Trump – US President

As much as I object to Trump's mindless self-promotion and gigantic ego, his statement above rings true for those of us who strive to improve our businesses and careers. Unfortunately, with instant electronic communication, we hear stories of **'overnight success'** that implies it's easy to be successful. Poor research, or maybe no research, lightweight and lazy journalism, and the perceived need for 'instant' gratification or success spreads this expectation. *Most of these overnight success stories are the result of years of hard work and sacrifice.* Think of J.K. Rowling, author of the *Harry Potter* books. As a single mother on social security benefits, she spent years writing in an Edinburgh café before her first novel was accepted.

The only example of instant success I can think of, apart from winning the lottery, is the story of Sir **Frank Packer, millionaire media owner and father of** the late media billionaire Kerry Packer[14]. The story goes that Sir Frank, in finding himself in an elevator of his Sydney office building along with a shabbily-dressed man in the 1960s, was outraged. Packer tells the man he's a disgrace to his firm, fires him, and hands him $1,000 to buy a new suit. The 'fired' man just grins. He's a freelance photographer who stopped by to visit a friend who worked in the building.

---

13   Attributed to Donald Trump, US President
14   See Chapter 6: Profits, section 1: Measures, part 1: Exit strategy...

Malcolm Gladwell, in *Outliers: The Story of Success,* **introduces** the concept of the **10,000-hour rule** where practice, hard work and opportunity will lead to success. This is where success is not due to the random distribution of genetic gifts or luck. He uses examples of The Beatles in music and Bill Gates with his computer software, whose success he attributes to the 10,000-hour rule of practice combined, to a much lesser extent, with opportunity.

Think of successful people around you, whether in business or in society. Almost always, their *success is the result of hard work and focus over many years.*

I can remember doing post-graduate studies, working a 12-hour day in a demanding job, with three children under five years old, and wondering whether it was worth the sacrifice for my wife and me. It was. It led onto lecturing at university, being headhunted for a job and, ultimately, into our own successful business.

As Donald Trump said 'who wants nothing?'

As I tell my children, 'The only place where *reward* **comes before** *work* **is in the** *dictionary.'*

4.2.3 Can see but am blind?

'If one can see things according to one's own belief system, one is destined to become virtually deaf, dumb and blind.'[15]
Robert Anton Wilson – author and futurist

How often, as managers, have we been unable to see what is *obvious and have been blinded by our own prejudices?*

---

15   Interview with Robert Anton Wilson by Jeffrey Elliott on 17 April 1980 in RAWilsonFans.org

Have you ever been looking for something and, even though you have been told where to look, you still cannot see the object even though it is in front of you?

This is because you have a **preconceived idea in your mind** of what you are looking for, so you subconsciously discount anything that does not meet the idea of what you are looking for.

I can remember quite clearly being blinded by my own prejudices while managing a trucking operation that distributed motor vehicles. Over several weeks, we had been receiving complaints of personal items being stolen from the vehicles. Initially, I was convinced that it was occurring in other state depots. The thefts continued and I still blamed the other depots. My fellow state managers implemented theft prevention strategies. The thefts continued and seemed to be increasing. Many of the items seemed to be of little value. The night supervision team claimed it was impossible that this could be occurring under their watch.

I was still convinced it was occurring elsewhere. Then one of my staff suggested that perhaps it was happening under our very own noses.

We set up a sting the next night, involving the police and a private investigator. Imagine my shock when two drivers working in our depot were caught stealing from a car on camera. All the time I had been blinded by my personal prejudices. The culprits, like the object in the cupboard, were there all the time.

This example demonstrates an important characteristic of good management.

Have you *reviewed all the possibilities*?

Have you *carefully considered them*?

Are you making *decisions based on emotions or pre-conceived ideas*?

4.2.4 Constant renewal – lessons from the farm

'Change and renewal are themes in life, aren't they?
We keep growing throughout life.'[16]

Susan Minot – American novelist

I grew up on a farm in New South Wales, Australia. In my opinion, it was one of the best groundings in life you can have. Many things observed and experienced as a child growing up on the farm can be related to business.

One experience that comes to mind is the problem of weeds.

On our farm, weeds, specifically burrs and thistles, were a major problem, and in particular a burr called the Bathurst Burr. Bathurst Burr is amongst the most common and economically serious weeds in Australian agriculture. It readily adheres to the wool of sheep. Wool contaminated by Bathurst Burrs is a substantial cost to the wool grower, as additional processing is required to separate the burrs from the wool. The burr was first introduced to the city of Bathurst, Australia's first settled inland city, in about 1850. It was trapped in the tails of horses imported from Valparaiso in Chile. Perhaps it should have been called the Chile Burr?

As my father was a woolgrower, Bathurst Burr was a major issue. As children, we were often sent out with a hoe to chip at the Bathurst Burr along the outside of the cultivation paddocks and roadsides. Call it character building. However, compared to other properties in the district, our farm had relatively small amounts of this burr.

Why was this so?

---

16 Interview with Susan Minot by Daniel Asa Rose on 6 March 2014 (Barnesandno-blereview.com)

It was not from our childhood efforts of chipping weeds along the roadside and in the paddocks. It was due to my dad who was constantly on the lookout for burrs. Whenever he saw a Bathurst Burr while horse riding, he would dismount from his horse and pull it out. As children, we were fascinated by this obsession of eradicating Bathurst Burrs and would often point them out to him if he missed one. This was very rare as, being an Aussie bushman, he had excellent eyesight.

By comparison, my school friend Graham, who also lived on a farm, had a different experience. His father's place had far more burrs than ours. Like my father, his father would often send him out chipping burrs. However, his father became ill, involving hospitalisation, and was unable to walk around his farm and keep burrs under control.

What was the difference?

The *constant attention* kept the burrs under control as my father would be watching for them on a daily basis.

This is the lesson for managers and business owners. Managing is not about platitudes, big schemes and projects. It is about *constant attention to detail*, continually seeking ways to improve every day.

What are the burrs in your organisation that need constant attention?

As a manager, *are you keeping these burrs under control?*

4.2.5 Other lessons from the farm...

'Farming looks mighty easy when your plough is a pencil and you're a thousand miles from the corn field.'[17]

Dwight D. Eisenhower – former US President

As mentioned in the last section, I grew up on a farm. This certainly gave me the experience and a *sense of perspective* to be successful, both academically and in business, and to handle difficult issues when they arose.

Being a farmer is more than a job, *it's a way of life*. It is full of life lessons that you can use as a manager or business owner. Farming is unpredictable. As a farmer, you are at the mercy of the weather whether it be droughts, storms or floods, as well as fluctuating commodity prices.

So what lessons can a farming life provide?

Here are three lessons from my childhood...

1. *Always be optimistic.* As a farmer, you tend to always look on the bright side of life, even when the problems seem insurmountable. Whether it's a crippling drought or a flood, or a tractor that breaks down in the middle of the sowing season, there is always tomorrow, next week or next year. I witnessed my father struggling financially to hand-feed sheep during a drought, believing that prices would improve. Later, wool prices increased and this made his efforts worthwhile.

---

17   Speech by US President Dwight Eisenhower at Bradley University, Illinois 25 September 1956

2. *Deal with disappointment.* Often, on the farm, despite
   your best efforts, things don't work out. The weather can
   be unpredictable, crops can be ruined, and animals can
   be lost to drought, flood or fire. This taught me that life
   is not easy, and you deal with disappointment by being
   resilient. You must keep going. In a period of severe
   drought, with no farm income and four hungry boys to
   feed, we dealt with this difficult period by my mother
   breeding corgi pups to sell to city people.

3. *You reap what you sow.* Despite the unpredictability
   of Mother Nature, in farming you generally get out
   of it what you put in. Proper preparation of the land
   before sowing a crop will be more likely to produce a
   successful crop. The lesson is that when you dedicate
   your time to doing a job correctly, without cutting
   corners, you are more likely to get your desired results.
   In business and in life, the results you get are based
   directly on the efforts you put into it. Over 40 years ago,
   my father saw a gap in the market for low-fat drought-
   hardy beef cattle. He began breeding Limousin cattle
   from France, initially through artificial insemination
   by using semen from the best French bulls. Within
   10 years, his cattle were winning national beef
   competitions in Australia.

*These lessons from the farm serve as good examples of good business
and life lessons.* Life is often not easy, whether with family, business
or your career. I found myself facing difficult issues in business – the
loss of a major customer, slow paying customers, staff issues. In one
year in our logistics business, we lost our two largest customers due to
circumstances beyond our control. This threatened the viability of the

business. It was similar to the farmer's livelihood being threatened by Mother Nature. We knuckled down, believed that the future would improve, dealt with the disappointment and worked hard at marketing our services. Within two years, our business had grown by 50%.

Can you think of examples where you overcame adversity and grew?

Do you think these three *lessons from the farm* are good examples on which to base action?

4.2.6 Never, never, never give in

'Never give in. Never give in. Never, never, never, never—
in nothing, great or small, large or petty—never give in,
except to convictions of honour and good sense.'[18]
Winston Churchill – British wartime Prime Minister

Winston Churchill was known for his inspiring speeches. Unlike most politicians today, he wrote many of his speeches himself. In business, as leaders and managers, we could do far worse than be inspired by some of Churchill's famous speeches.

Never giving in?

Often, in the face of adversity, it is easier to not make the extra effort to achieve the outcome required. As I reflect on my journey of establishing and managing a business, Churchill's 'never give in' speech resonates.

Back when our business was just starting out, we were given a three-month contract with a major Australian retailer to manage their Christmas overflow. This effectively doubled our existing business and would have prevented the business from failing. After

---

18   Address by Winston Churchill to Harrow School on 29 October 1941

we had signed the contract, we then received a phone call saying, 'Sorry, we've decided not to use you.'

Large Australian retailers are notoriously ruthless when dealing with suppliers, especially small ones. Although we had a contract, we were in no financial position to seek redress for them breaking it. If we had taken legal action, we would have been out of business before the matter was addressed and we could not afford it anyway. With our backs to the wall, we went back and negotiated successfully with the retailer's distribution centre manager, convincing him that the honourable action was to adhere to the contract. This gave us our first big start in the business.

Several years later, our largest customer owed us a six-figure sum and was reluctant to pay. Failure to pay would have meant the collapse of our business unless we were able to secure a bank loan to cover working capital. This was something we were reluctant to do, as our houses had been mortgaged to establish the business. Negotiations were not fruitful in reducing the debt owed to us and we became extremely worried. We kept the pressure up without success. Luckily, the customer decided to cease using our services, but they needed to move their stock. This presented the leverage we needed to get paid. Put simply, 'no payment, no stock'. Our business was saved and 12 months later, the former customer went bankrupt.

Successfully selling our business was our last example of 'never, never, never give in'. After two failed sales attempts in 12 months[19], it looked as though the business would never be sold. We would not receive a reward for over 15 years of hard work and worry. Seven prospective business brokers were interviewed to assist in selling the business and were rejected for one reason or another. It looked like another failure. However, I encouraged one of the brokers to try

---

19   See Chapter 6: Profits, section 1: Measures, part 1: Exit strategy...

another approach. After weeks of trying to convince all my partners to use his company's services, he was appointed to sell the business. This proved decisive. The broker had international experience and was able to sell the business to an international buyer, exceeding our expectations.

In business, as in management, **staying power or persistence will often win out in the end,** sometimes when you least expect it.

Do you have examples of where 'never never never' giving in has brought unexpected results?

Was it worth the effort?

4.2.7 Three things my mother taught me about business...

'My mother taught me to appreciate a job well done –
"If you're going to kill each other do it outside –
I have just finished cleaning!"'
Anonymous

In Australia, Mother's Day is the second Sunday in May. This is the day where you thank your mother and reflect on what a wonderful person she is. Apart from appreciating a job well done, what else did your mother teach you?

As business owners and managers, *can we learn from our mothers?*

My mother was a school teacher, a city girl who married a farmer in rural New South Wales in the 1950s. This was probably not the life her father, a senior public servant, had envisaged for his youngest daughter. Perhaps this background helped her teach her sons about life.

Here are three things my mother taught me that have helped me in business.

1. **Strong work ethic**

   My earliest memories of my mother were of her looking after her four sons and making significant sacrifices. Mum went back to work when my youngest brother went to school, primarily because her income would help support and educate our family. The uncertainties of rural life with droughts and low commodity prices meant 'off farm' income was essential. She would drive off every day to teach, come home, do her domestic chores and then plan and mark schoolwork well into the night. This hard work had its own rewards – providing an education for her sons, the satisfaction of educating and inspiring the children she taught and providing financial stability for the family. *With a clear goal in mind, there is no substitute in business for hard work.*

2. **Perseverance**

   Folk singer Eric Bogle's song 'Now I'm Easy' depicts rural life as being often hard and an unrelenting grind:

   Of droughts and fires and floods I've lived through plenty
   This country's dust and mud have seen my tears and blood.

   Through the heat, droughts, low prices, flies and dust, Mum persevered in supporting Dad and providing physical, emotional and moral support to the family. Mum would say, 'Put your back into it and keep going.' I've taken this thinking into business. Even if the worst appears to have occurred, stay calm, focus and carry on. *Don't sweat the small stuff, and don't get caught up in the crisis. With focus and hard work, it will pass.*

3. **Fierce self-reliance**

My mother was fiercely hard working, independent and had a strong sense of self-belief, often introducing new ideas into a conservative rural community. She instilled in all her sons these qualities of independence and self-reliance with a strong emphasis on the value of education. When you're young and starting out in a new job or a new business, it can be hard to remember, in the face of critics, *how important self-reliance is.*

So, on Mother's Day, think about what your mother taught you when you were growing up and thank her. Mum's qualities taught us to trust in our decisions and not hide from our mistakes.

As Mum would say, 'It's not the mistakes you make, but how you deal with them.'

This implied that *a high work ethic, perseverance and fierce self-reliance would see you through.*

As a business owner or manager, what did your mother teach you? Can these lessons be used in your business or career?

4.2.8 What were the management lessons from the Battle of the Somme?

'Lions led by donkeys.'[20]
Erich Ludendorff – German World War I general

This quote is attributed to General Eric Ludendorff, describing the British tactics in the Battle of the Somme in France in World War I.

---

20 Attributed to World War I German General Erich Ludendorff although the original source remains in dispute

The battle lasted for over four months in 1916 and resulted in almost **624,000 casualties**:

- **146,431** British Commonwealth and French Allies deaths
- **164,907** German deaths.

It became a potent symbol of *the futility of war*, where the 'flower of British manhood' was lost, and *a byword for incompetent leadership*.

The plan was to break the German trenches through a week-long arterial bombardment – destroying the German trench system, including the barbed wire protecting the German trenches and the trench's occupants, and neutralise the German artillery. The Allied infantry would then advance in waves through 'no man's land' with little or no resistance and take the German positions.

However, the plan failed in its main objectives.

Why?

The German troops were too well dug in and low-level clouds prevented aerial artillery spotting. It had also been confidently assumed that the shells would destroy the German barbed wire in front of their trenches. Unfortunately, it was only partially successful and left 'no man's land' a tangle of barbed wire and craters that made it difficult for the advancing infantry to negotiate. After the bombardment, the Germans emerged from their bunkers and met the advancing infantry with well-placed machine guns.

Were there other reasons?

Yes, more importantly, many of the artillery rounds were *duds*. An estimated 30% *failed to explode or were the wrong type of projectile*. This led to the barbed wire remaining largely intact. Furthermore, much of the bombardment was shrapnel shells, not high explosives, and the shells failed to make enough impact to blow away the wire or damage the deep enemy dugouts.

What caused the high level of dud artillery shells?

World War I was an industrial war. Massive amounts of material were required shells, ammunition, ships, railways and aircraft, as well as kitting out millions of combatants. In 1916, after two years of war Britain was running short of artillery shells. To meet the demand, many companies who had no experience in manufacturing munitions began production. While manufacturing shells may not be difficult, it was a different story with fuses. Fuses were technically difficult to manufacture and therefore the quality suffered. Quality controls in the expanded munitions industry were poor. It is also difficult to expand production capability rapidly without quality issues. This was exacerbated by worn gun barrels, which contributed to shells not landing fuse first and exploding. Over 1.5 million shells were fired in the first week, many of them duds. Most of the faulty fuses were tracked to a single manufacturer. Remedial action was quickly taken and the problem was resolved progressively after the Battle of the Somme.

What were some of the other reasons?

Although *technology was a major factor*, it was further exacerbated by *incompetent leadership* and *strict adherence to a flawed and untested strategy*.

General Haig, the British commander, had never visited the front to see the effects of the bombardment and later the massive loss of life. A patrol into 'no man's land' the night before the Allied infantry were to advance reported that the barbed wire had not been destroyed. *This report was ignored.* Low-level clouds prevented aircraft from spotting this problem. Other patrols into 'no man's land' reported hearing the Germans singing in their trenches indicating the barrage had failed in its objectives and was also ignored. Other factors were the inexperience and immature state of training of the officers and artillery gunners.

Should Haig and his staff have done something different once they knew the bombardment had been only partially effective?

Could they have avoided the tens of thousands of casualties of the opening attack?

It is easy in retrospect to believe that they could have.

However, the Commonwealth forces faced an impossible situation. Their major ally the French, were pushing hard for the British to launch an attack to prevent the destruction of the French Army in the Battle of Verdun, by reducing the German forces pitted against them. There had also been no opportunity for surprise, and with the artillery barrage, the Germans knew that the attack was coming.

What could they have done?

Cancel or delay the attack? Yes, this was possible.

Fire an even longer bombardment? This was not practical due to a shortage of shells, as well as dud or incorrect shells, so the die was cast.

It was easy to be wise in hindsight.

So, what are the management lessons from the Battle of the Somme?

1. *Do NOT overly rely on technology* – technology is an enabler and not the answer[21]

2. *Quality control and competent supervision is essential* in organisations, as demonstrated by poor management in the factories[22]

---

21   See Chapter 5: Productivity, section 1: History, part 2: Technology
22   See Chapter 4: Processes, section 3: Lessons, part 5: Process improvement

3. *Incompetent leadership severely impacts on organisations.*
    Over 150,000 Allied deaths could have been prevented
    if the facts had not been ignored. This was further
    complicated by not having a Plan B[23], using an unproven
    strategy, not having enough equipment and not doing
    their homework[24].

There are *valuable lessons* for managers in learning from *military blunders*.

Can you think of examples in your work life or in your organisation where the over reliance on **technology, poor supervision** and **quality control** severely impacted an organisation?

Elephants are afraid of bees

---

23 See Chapter 3: Planning, section 2: Roadmap, part 3: What is your plan?
24 See Chapter 4: Processes, section 3: Lessons, part 2: Doing your homework

4.3
LESSONS

4.3.1 Above the line and below the line thinking...

'We can complain because rose bushes have thorns or rejoice because thorn bushes have roses.'[25]

Abraham Lincoln – former US President

There is another important concept that I would like to introduce, *above and below the line thinking*.

This is a very powerful concept, *'The Line'* is the parallel that divides our character and represents responsibility and accountability. **Responsibility** is a very important word. A true leader takes responsibility for their team and helps them achieve goals. It is a powerful life skill that puts into practice the act of ownership, taking responsibility and being **accountable** for your actions. Being accountable means that you are responsible and answerable for your actions.

Acting **below the line**, our lives become circumstance-driven. They include the characteristics of laying blame, denial and making excuses.

---

25   Attributed to President Lincoln but appears in book *A Tour of My Garden* by Jean-Baptiste Karr, a French critic, journalist and novelist

ABOVE THE LINE THINKING

Ownership

Accountability

Responsibility

BELOW THE LINE THINKING

Blame

Excuses

Denial

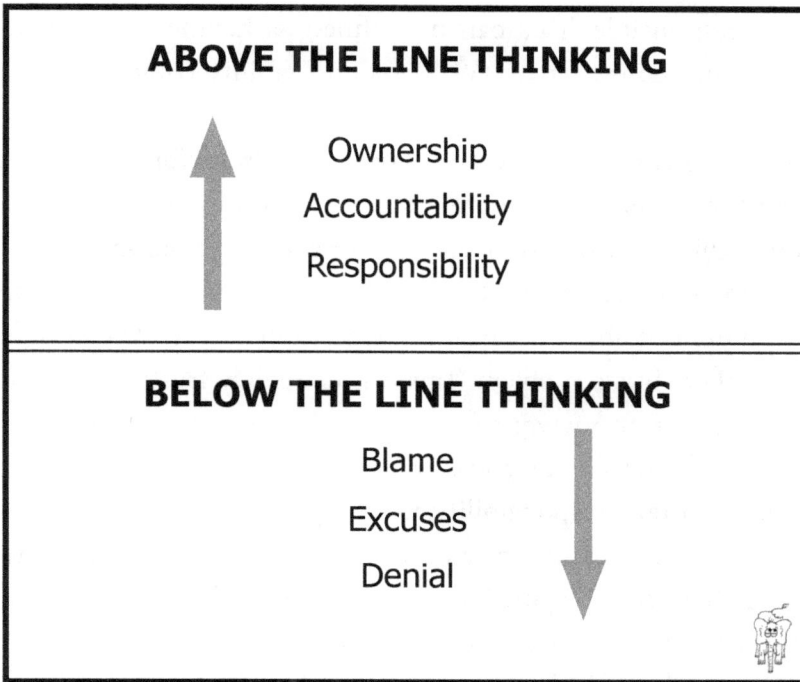

Figure 8: Above and Below the Line Thinking

Are you a **victor** or **victim**?

Laying blame is far too common in organisations and businesses whether it is the CEO or others. It shows that they are not willing to be accountable or responsible for their actions. Excuses don't solve the issues or promote responsibility. They usually cause frustration.

When in denial, we are committing yet another below the line action – 'I didn't do it.' This obviously ineffective response can create certain frustration in others and make us appear unreliable and dishonest.

Victims let things happen to them, do not take control, are pessimistic, find reasons why not and always appear tired and stressed.

By choosing to act **above the line** we are using **'response-ability'** – that is taking responsibility for your performance and showing you can be responsible. This can be defined as having the ability to respond and be proactive. With response-ability comes increasing choices and freedoms that we may have never had before.

By living **above the line**, you take responsibility for your own life, business or career. You begin to have greater control because you stop blaming things outside yourself for your current situation.

I remember being in a business where a manager always came up with excuses about poor business performance while continuing to deny there was a problem. This was extremely frustrating for me. It began to affect my work performance and emotional state. I was blaming him rather than taking ownership for my performance. I decided to take responsibility for my performance and the business's performance. This filtered down the organisation to others, making them take responsibility for their sections. Unsurprisingly, performance improved and so did workplace morale.

Responsibility is the ability to respond to the events that happen in our lives. When you sit back and accept things that happen to you, you are allowing the circumstances of life to control you rather than taking control of those circumstances. *When you take action, you make life happen for you, not to you.*

Pushing responsibility and authority downwards is one of the six strategies that Sam Walton identifies in *Sam Walton: Made in America* as making Walmart a successful business.

What situations have you faced where you have blamed circumstances instead of taking ownership and responsibility yourself?

Would you now take a different action?

4.3.2 Doing your homework

'All of us, at certain moments of our lives, need to take advice and to receive help from other people.'[26]

Alexis Carrel – French Nobel Prize for Medicine winner

How often in your work or business life have you *not done your homework* and put yourself under unnecessary pressure?

An incident many years ago very clearly demonstrated that I had not done my homework. When working in the concrete industry, while sitting in my office in Melbourne, I thought I could prepare a capital expenditure application for an environmental washing system at a concrete plant located in regional Victoria.

There had been great reluctance from head office to fix the environmental problem of disposing of concrete waste. I gathered 'letters of protest' from neighbours, one of whom was an employee who lived behind the plant. Upon touring the area with my general manager several weeks later, he brought out the application, stood near where I had said the washing plant was to be located and started asking questions. This was a very trying time as the document explained where the wastewater was running and it was uphill. Obviously not immediately obvious from my office in Melbourne.

I learnt two valuable lessons:

1. Do your homework
2. There is no substitute for physically being on site (management by walking around[27]).

---

26 Attributed to Alexis Carrel, French scientist Nobel Prize winner and promoter of eugenics

27 See Chapter 5: Productivity, section 2: Change, part 2: Management by walking around

However, even *the largest companies fail to do their homework*. Several years ago, Rio Tinto, a major international mining company, was forced to write down $3 billion because their plan to barge coal down the Zambezi River in Mozambique was not physically possible, and required government approval to dredge the river. Perhaps they could have learnt from history. David Livingstone, the famous African missionary and explorer, was unable to navigate up the Zambezi in a small craft due to the Cahora Bassa rapids. The Rio Tinto managing director lost his job primarily over this debacle.

Years later, in our logistics business, we had to convert a casual warehouse lease to a permanent lease. We were nervous that our landlord would want both a long-term commitment and an increase in rent. The previous week, our warehouse manager advised us that the owner had been on-site several times over the past month with 'unknown' persons in suits. There had been some cosmetic tidying up and painting undertaken on external parts of the building.

I did some more homework and discovered that the landlord was seeking to sell the property and needed a permanent lease to interest a possible purchaser. This information changed the dynamics of the negotiations. We were able to negotiate a rent under market value, with shorter fixed terms and lower annual increases, and the owner was delighted – a real win/win.

Remember: there is *no substitute for doing your homework* thoroughly.

The elephant is the national animal of Thailand

4.3.3 Another lesson from the farm...

'There's nothing like putting your bare feet into fresh cow dung on a cold day. It's great.'[28]

Makhaya Ntini – first ethnically black cricketer to play for South Africa

Here is another **'farm story'** from my childhood. One of my jobs was to 'pen up the calf' each evening. This was done so that when my father milked the calf's mother in the morning, the cow would have enough milk for our growing family of four boys. Rounding up the calf each evening was often a challenge. Regularly, the calf would be cunning and refuse to go through the gate to be penned up.

The cow paddock was also a world of excitement for young boys. A creek to cross, dive bombing plovers in mating season, the odd angry bull, a mob of kangaroos with joeys, snakes...

What a challenge.

However, the **paddock had other dangers.** Yes, it was full of **'land mines'**, our nickname for cow manure ranging from the very fresh to the dry and dusty.

It was fun to trick my youngest brother. He sometimes followed me around on my afternoon chores. On one of his first adventures into the paddock with me to pen up the calf for the night, I encouraged him to jump on a week-old cow pat. Not being entirely convinced, he tapped it with a stick. It sounded hard so he then, with my encouragement, jumped on it.

Two things happened.

Firstly, he was shin deep in cow manure and secondly, I doubled up with laughter, apparently the look on my brother's face said it all. What a mean older brother. I certainly had some explaining to do to my mother when we got home.

---

28   As reported in The Cricket Monthly (*www.thecricketmonthly.com*) on 31 January 2018

The cow paddock, in many ways, was a great learning ground for a life in business.

It was a very practical lesson – **'what you see is not always what you get'**

What are your **land mines**?

Are you careful enough in **assessing opportunities** and **problems?** [29]

Are they what they seem on the surface? [30]

4.3.4 Blitzkrieg – what are the management lessons?

'You can't outrun the future if you don't see it coming.
Individuals who get startled by the future weren't
paying attention.' [31]

Gary Hamel – American management expert and Visiting Professor at Harvard Business School

What is blitzkrieg?

Blitzkrieg, roughly translated from German, means 'lightning war' and was a method of warfare used by Nazi Germany when successfully invading northern Europe in World War II[32]. At the beginning of World War II, France had the largest army in Europe with the most tanks and aircraft. However, in 1940, they were defeated comprehensibly by the Nazi war machine in a matter of weeks. To be successful, Nazi Germany did not fight France on *their terms* or in *more traditional ways*. Instead, they used *'blitzkrieg'*.

---

29 See Chapter 4: Processes, section 1: Essentials, part 5: SWOT analysis
30 See Chapter 4: Processes, section 1 Essentials, part 3: The 5 Whys
31 Attributed to Gary Hamel, author and business thinker
32 *Note:* the use of Blitzkrieg as an example of a management technique and is not to be misinterpreted as support for the evil actions of Nazi Germany which resulted in over 30 million deaths in World War II.

So, how did the Germans successfully invade France in World War II?

Following World War I, the French built a series of defensive forts on their eastern frontier with Germany called the Maginot Line, to protect them against invasion. Although outnumbered, the Germans used a combination of tanks, motorised infantry and aircraft in a combined offensive mobile approach, using excellent radio communications. They bypassed the Maginot Line and attacked France through the Ardennes, which the French had considered 'tank-proof'.

By comparison, the French relied on static forts and viewed tanks as a defensive weapon to support their infantry. Few of the heavy tanks had radios and they were also unreliable.

What are the lessons from blitzkrieg that can be used in business?

In summary, it was 'old war' vs 'new war' and broke the 'old thinking'.

The German approach meant *challenging the traditional ways* by doing things differently which required planning to get around a superior enemy, without fighting on the enemy's terms, and by using:

- Speed and efficiency – mobile infantry and tanks supported by aircraft
- New technology – extensive use of radios.

There are many examples of companies who failed to change, resulting in their demise. For example, although Kodak invented the digital camera, it failed to commercialise it. Nokia, the leading mobile phone business at the time, invented the smartphone, however its delay in commercialising meant the company was overtaken by Apple and Samsung.

I had a client whose business relied on providing engineering services to a major vehicle manufacturer in Australia for the majority of its revenue. The owner proudly told me that he could always rely on this company as he had dealt with them for over 30 years. Within two years of this statement, vehicle manufacturing ceased and his business folded.

As business owners and managers, we must always be thinking of new ways of doing things[33], embracing new technologies and seeking outside assistance where appropriate.

Here are *three questions* you can ask yourself:

1. How can I get customers from my competitors but *not compete on the same terms?*
2. Where is my business *vulnerable to new technologies?*
3. Are any of my new or existing competitors *competing differently* in the market?

This is your challenge.

After all, *ignoring emerging trends or becoming overly absorbed in the present is naïve or even reckless.*

---

33   See Chapter 4: Processes, section 2: Methods, part 4: Constant renewal – lessons from the farm

4.3.5 Process improvement

'Without continual growth and progress, such words as improvement, achievement, and success have no meaning.'[34]

Benjamin Franklin – one of the Founding Fathers of the USA

Against a background of continual distractions, including increasing regulations and competition, one of the *greatest challenges for businesses is to continue improve their performance and profitability.* Improved processes lead to better efficiencies, improved productivity, greater employee satisfaction and, ultimately profits.

At its most basic level, there are four ways to improve productivity:

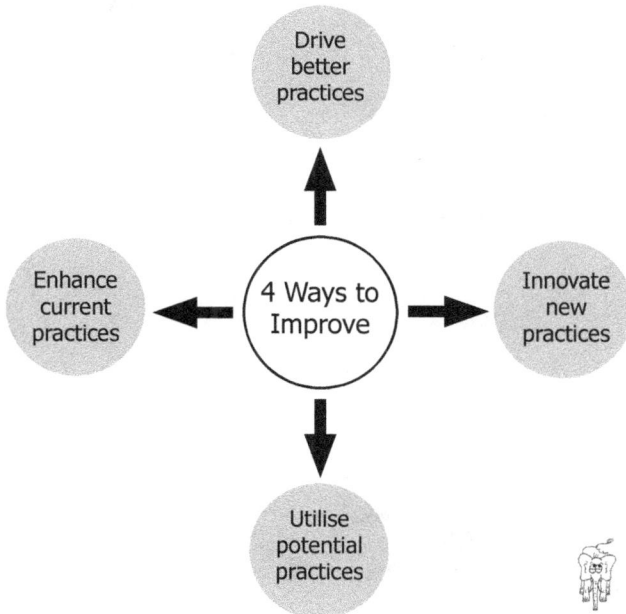

Figure 9: Four Ways to Improve

34　Attributed to Benjamin Franklin, author, inventor and US statesman and Founding Father of the USA

In Japan, following the devastation of World War II, the concept of 'quality management' was developed and implemented by an American, W. Edward Deming. He became known as the 'father of quality management' and his work led to the amazing success of Japanese companies such as Toyota, Sony and Mitsubishi. The 'Deming management method' became known as the Plan-Do-Study-Act (PDSA) cycle, which imbedded learning into a cycle of continous improvement[35].

Figure 10: Plan-Do-Study-Act (PDSA) Cycle

---

35   More in-depth information on the 'Deming method' of quality management can be found online and in various publications.

The aims of this section are to:

1. Describe how important process improvement is to a business
2. Introduce a methodology we used to improve productivity in our logistics business.

Our third-party logistics business's specific niche was retail logistics. When the business was first set up, it provided floor-ready merchandising services (FRM©) to retail suppliers. At that stage, the business was not a traditional warehousing and transport business, instead stock was processed in the warehouse in a way that enabled it to be placed in each individual retail store in a 'floor-ready' condition, underpinned by an electronic commerce system. Items were price and security labelled, placed on hangers if required and scan-packed to store level.

This required a more varied skill set than traditional warehousing. The production process depended on the type of merchandise – whether apparel, shoes, cosmetics or electronics. This required a flexible approach and a standard methodology. Each supervisor would organise and 'set up' the job, and plan and manage the FRM© process. The productivity of each job and section was measured[36] and reviewed individually with the supervisors on a weekly basis.

The methodology was called 'the W5H Check' because it asked *why, what, where, when, who and how*. Before each job was set up, the supervisor used this checklist to maximise productivity by answering the questions on the checklist as shown in Figure 11. This approach improved productivity by reducing the number of times the goods

---

36   See Chapter 4: Processes, section 1: Essentials, part 6: Measuring and Chapter 5: Productivity, section 2: Change, part 1: What is a KPI?

How to Eliminate Unnecessary Tasks
(and combine or rearrange the sequence to SIMPLIFY the operation)

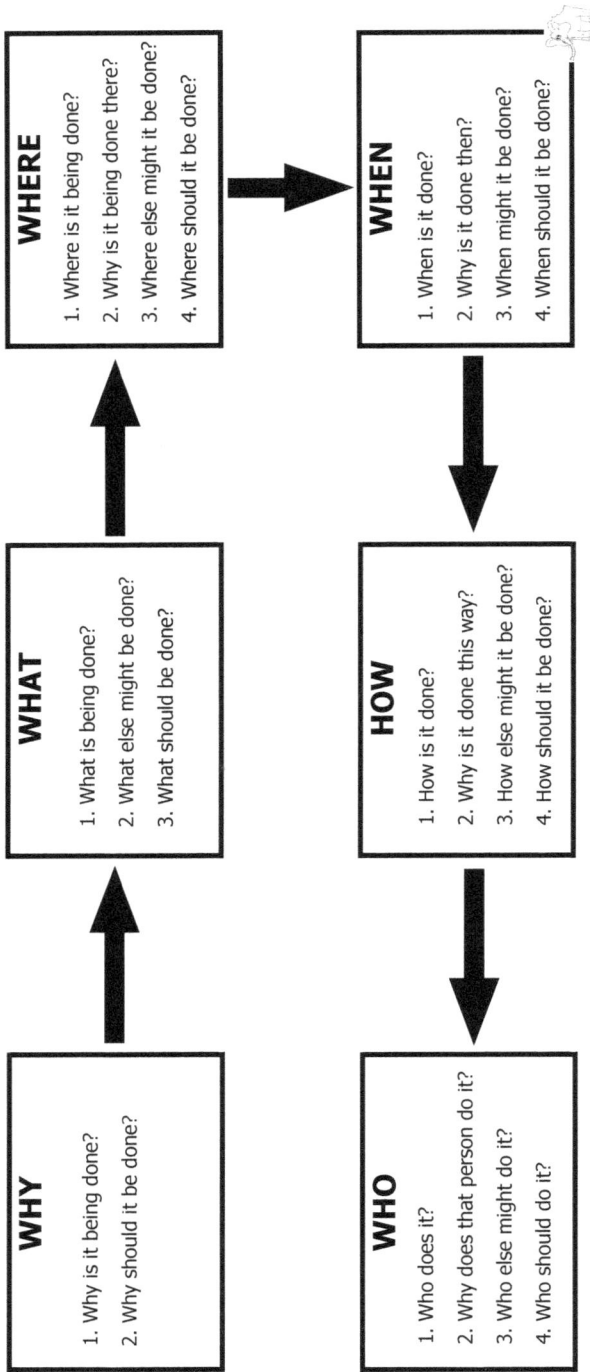

WHY

1. Why is it being done?
2. Why should it be done?

WHAT

1. What is being done?
2. What else might be done?
3. What should be done?

WHERE

1. Where is it being done?
2. Why is it being done there?
3. Where else might it be done?
4. Where should it be done?

WHEN

1. When is it done?
2. Why is it done then?
3. When might it be done?
4. When should it be done?

HOW

1. How is it done?
2. Why is it done this way?
3. How else might it be done?
4. How should it be done?

WHO

1. Who does it?
2. Why does that person do it?
3. Who else might do it?
4. Who should do it?

Figure 11: W5H Check©

were handled, minimising lifting and walking, questioning who was doing the work, eliminating unnecessary tasks and simplifying the process.

We found that this *process improved productivity over time as it was decentralised, empowered the supervisors to make decisions*, and *measured performance*. The supervisors were encouraged to seek input from their staff on how best to improve productivity and were authorised to communicate directly with the customers. It was similar to the PDSA cycle used in the Deming method and included specific questions that required thought. The W5H Check© sparked a *process of continous improvement* that was driven by 'hands-on' supervisors who were given the authority to make decisions that were the best for the customer and for the business.

The benefits of this system included very low staff and supervisor turnover, long-term customer retention and high levels of employee satisfaction. When the business was sold, the majority of supervisors had been with the company for over 10 years.

What are the areas in your business that you could improve using the simple Four Ways to Improve test as shown in Figure 9?

Do you think that the W5H Check© system would be useful in improving productivity in your business?

Are there *lessons to be learnt from the example above*, relating to pushing responsibility down to supervisor level?

Elephants cannot become drunk on the fruit of the marula tree .

4.3.6 What were the management lessons from the Battle of Britain?

'Never in the field of human conflict was so much owed by so many to so few.'[37]

Winston Churchill – British wartime Prime Minister

In the Battle of Britain, the history books champion the heroics of the fighter squadrons of the RAF in defeating the German Luftwaffe. Churchill sought to reinforce this view through his famous quote about 'the few', being the fighter pilots of the RAF Fighter Command. The reasons for the British victory were *far more complex*.

The Battle of Britain commenced soon after the fall of France on 25th June 1940 and ended in October of the same year. The German strategy was to obtain air superiority over Britain before Operation Sealion, Hitler's invasion of Britain. The Luftwaffe had over three times more attacking aircraft, bombers and fighters than the RAF Fighter Command. When the Battle ended, the Luftwaffe had lost nearly 2,000 aircraft and over 2,600 airmen, compared to the RAF who lost over 1,000 aircraft and just over 530 airmen.

So, how did the RAF succeed against such odds?

There were several *interrelated reasons*, including the German fighters flying at the end of their range, the use of radar by the British, poor German intelligence, the bravery and skill of the RAF pilots, higher attrition of German pilots compared to the British, the weather, and the confused and changing German strategy.

The German strategy, for example, changed from attacking the ports and English Channel convoys to destroying the RAF, either on

---

37   Address by Prime Minister Winston Churchill to House of Commons on 20 August 1940

the ground or in the air, and then later bombing the cities and industrial sites in southern England. Furthermore, the German Luftwaffe, headed by Hermann Göring, was both autocratic and bureaucratic.

However, *the prime reason is considered to have been the tactics initiated by Air Marshall Hugh Dowding*, through the *use of new technology, radar and a flexible command structure* called the Dowding system. This moulded together technology, ground defences and fighter aircraft. Interestingly, the Blitzkrieg's initial success[38] can be attributed to using technology and a flexible command structure.

Britain was divided into four geographical areas called 'fighter groups' and then further divided into 'sectors'. Each 'sector' had a fighter airfield with an operations room from where the fighters could be directed. As radar tracked the incoming Luftwaffe raids, information was sent to group headquarters, then to the 'sectors' where fighters would be scrambled, and air defence stations notified, all in a short period of time. This strategy allowed the RAF to engage the enemy **selectively** and in a **timely way**.

The RAF fighters did not engage German fighters unless they were escorting bombers. The Hurricane fighters attacked the incoming German bombers and the Spitfire fighters waited for the bombers to turn for France before attacking both fighters and bombers. This was when the Germans had little fuel or ammunition left. It is a common misconception that the Spitfires and Hurricanes were offensive weapons. They weren't. They were *defensive interceptors* with the sole purpose of intercepting bombers on the way in to prevent them from carrying out their mission and hunting them down when they turned back home to France. The German *bombers* were the attack weapons – attacking industrial centres, cities, shipping and ports.

---

38 See Chapter 4: Processes, section 3: Lessons, part 4: Blitzkrieg – what are the management lessons?

What can we learn for business from the Battle of Britain?

There are potentially *three management lessons* from the Battle of Britain.

1. *Flexible management systems* are better than authoritarian and bureaucratic systems.

   Kodak, who initially invented the digital camera, failed to commercialise it successfully. Flexible management systems that are agile will beat bureaucratic organisations every time[39]. In another example, we were able to contribute to the success of our logistics business by empowering supervisors to communicate directly with their assigned customers. This not only improved customer service but developed the supervisory and management skills of the supervisor.

2. *Technology is only an enabler.*

   Airbnb's software has 'enabled' a new source of cheaper accommodation for travellers through the letting of private rooms and apartments that were not previously considered available. Here, technology was the enabler. Another example, our logistics business was created from an opportunity when a major Australian retailer changed its supply chain systems, forcing suppliers to prepare their products in a store-floor ready condition. The enabler was a technology called electronic data interchange or EDI, as it allowed for more efficient management of the supply chain[40].

---

39 See Chapter 4: Processes, section 2: Methods, part 8: What are the management lessons from the Battle of the Somme?

40 See Chapter 5: Productivity, section 1: History, part 2: Technology

3. *Engage on your own terms.*

Too often, business owners try to be all things to all people. They do not focus on their strengths or find a niche and end up competing against larger and better-resourced competitors. Yellowtail Wines[41] was a small family-owned Australian wine company who created a new market for wine for unsophisticated and new wine drinkers in US, and avoided head-to-head confrontation with the major industry players. They engaged on their own terms where they saw they had a competitive advantage. In our logistics business, we targeted, to great success, smaller owner-operated companies who did not want to deal with large impersonal national organisations.

As managers and business owners, what are the valuable lessons learnt from the Battle of Britain that you can use in our own business? There are *valuable lessons* for managers in *studying history…*

There are elephants in Ethiopia

---

41   https://www.thebrandingjournal.com/2014/05/yellow-tail-clever-product-positioning-within-american-wine-industry

4.3.7 What can a Sherlock Holmes story teach us about management?

'My name is Sherlock Holmes. It is my business to know what other people don't know.'[42]

Sherlock Holmes – fictional English detective

As business owners and managers, we are often concentrating on 'the business noise' and daily work activities rather than what is *not* happening in the business. *The Sherlock Holmes mystery, The Adventure of Silver Blaze*, involving the apparent murder of a champion race horse's trainer and the disappearance of the racehorse, illustrates this point.

On the night of the alleged crime, the residents in the house near the stables heard no sound.

The dialogue from the book makes interesting reading:

Inspector Gregory (Scotland Yard detective): *'Is there any other point to which you would wish to draw my attention?'*[43]

Sherlock Holmes: *'To the curious incident of the dog in the night-time.'*

Inspector Gregory: *'The dog did nothing in the night-time.'*

Sherlock Holmes: *'That was the curious incident.'*

What was Holmes' conclusion?

As dogs often bark at strangers and the dog did not bark, perhaps the offender lived in the house near the stables. This important clue, 'the dog didn't bark' helped Sherlock Holmes solve the mystery.

What can we learn from Holmes' actions in *The Adventure of Silver Blaze?*

---

42 Arthur Conan Doyle, *The Adventure of the Blue Carbuncle,* 1892
43 Arthur Conan Doyle, *The Adventure of the Silver Blaze,* 1892

We normally think that important clues involve events *that did happen*. However, we often forget that events *that did not happen* can be more important.

Using customer service as an example, we concentrate on replying to customer phone calls and emails, whereas instead *we should also be concentrating on those customers we do not hear from*, the equivalent of the dog that did not bark.

The customer could be very satisfied or extremely unhappy with our products and services.

Reconnecting with the customer presents us with a *great opportunity* to reinforce the positive experience they are having with our service or products, or to save their business from going to competitors because of a poor experience.

My involvement in a start-up business illustrates this point. We had been advised by management that the customer experience was excellent, although our sales figures did not reflect this fact. We then contacted customers and potential customers and found that our communication processes were inadequate and needed urgent attention. There had been no 'business noise', the dog did not bark.

Are you looking at what is *not happening* regarding staff and customers, especially those you do not hear from?[44]

This may provide valuable clues on where to improve products, services, staff relations or management style.

---

44 See Chapter 5: Productivity, section 3: Consistency, part 5: Recognising poorly managed organisations

5
PRODUCTIVITY

The fourth 'P' is productivity. We have now decided on the best method for cooking and eating the elephant. The challenge now is to determine the most efficient way of doing this.

What equipment or technology do we need? What are the tasks that need to be done? What is the most efficient use of people and other resources to cook the elephant?

Are there tasks that are not necessary or are inefficient? Do the hide and tusks need to be separated from the rest of the elephant, as there is no point cooking these parts because they are inedible?

Do the knives need to be sharpened to cut up the elephant?

5.1
HISTORY

5.1.1 Déjà vu all over again

The following advertisement for the International Commercial Truck, circa 1910, is on display in Maine's Owls Head Transportation Museum:

> That the motor truck is an excellent substitute for the horse has been proven in every instance where businessmen have given it a fair trial. But the man who uses his motor truck simply as a substitute for horses neglects to make the most of his opportunities. The horse is not a machine – five to six hours' actual work – fifteen to twenty-five miles – is its maximum day's work. A motor truck can be used twenty-four hours a day if necessary, and it will travel the last hour and the hundredth mile just as fast as the first. Businessmen who are using the motor truck in place of the horse and wagon equipment with the greatest success are men who have given this problem careful study. In most instances it was necessary to change the plan of routing – delays which were necessary to give horses rest were eliminated – plans were laid to keep the truck busy the entire day with as few delays as possible...

The use of new technology is the key to increasing productivity. However, *pre-conceived ideas* or *environmental pre-conditioning* of our thoughts often *prevent us from realising the potential of new technology.*

There are some great examples. With the advent of the motor car in the late 19th century in England, the Locomotive Act 1865, otherwise known as the Red Flag Act, stipulated that self-propelled vehicles have a man with a red flag or lantern walking at least 60 yards (55 metres) ahead of each vehicle at walking pace to warn horse riders and horse-drawn traffic of the approach of the vehicle. When visiting my son in Japan, I had to wait until 10am for the ATM to open, which was when banks opened, to access my bank account. Neither of these examples make practical sense.

In an earlier role as a transport manager, I was confronted by the long-distance truck drivers I was managing. They told me that each driver must have their own truck, even though it was owned by their employer. This limited the distance that could be travelled per week to less than 3,500km, due to legal driving hour restrictions and the driver physically being unable to safely drive further each week. Breaking this thinking was difficult. However, multi-driver trucks were introduced, with drivers rostered according to the legal driving hours and the trucks operating 24 hours per day for over six days per week. The average distance travelled per truck exceeded 9,000km per week, with some trucks doing 12,000km. This high truck utilisation resulted in a significant increase in company profitability, as fixed costs were covered early in the working week. Correspondingly, the number of kilometres per driver increased. As they were paid according to distance travelled, they were winners too.

The *challenge for managers is to do away with preconceived ideas based on history and experience,* and objectively look at where new technology can increase productivity and lower costs. My former accountants continued to increase their charges each year, charging me for postage when they could have emailed me documents, charging my business a direct debit fee for paying our account rather than sending a cheque, and so on. When I queried why our fees kept on increasing, I was told it was because their costs kept on increasing. Clearly, they were not passing on the savings of implementing new technology and were trapped in the 'old way' of thinking. Not only did they lose our business, but they also lost our logistics business' work and the directors' work as well. Interestingly, they did not follow up why they had lost this work.

Are you trapped in your 'old ways'?

Are working in your business rather than on it?

Remember: *change is inevitable* and *what we did yesterday will not be good enough for tomorrow.* If you don't recognise this, I can guarantee that your competitors will.

5.1.2 Technology

'Men have become the tools of their tools.'[1]

Henry David Thoreau – American philosopher and historian

In business today, we are confronted with a mass of technological innovation that has become increasingly more sophisticated, expensive and difficult to keep up with – iPhones, iPads, tablets, GPS, and so on. *We often become so intoxicated with new technology – its speed, power, gadgetry and the potential to solve our business problems – that we neglect to solve problems in a simple and cost-effective way.*

Have you heard of the story about NASA's astronauts finding that pens would not work in space in the 1960s?

NASA spent tens of thousands of dollars to develop a space pen while the Russian cosmonauts used a pencil. This is an 'urban myth', but it illustrates the need to try and solve problems in a simple, practical and cost-effective way.

---

1   Henry David Thoreau, *Walden, or Life in the Woods,* 1854

In the first Gulf War, the fleeing Iraqi army set fire to hundreds of oil wells, creating an environmental disaster. Red Adair, the famous Texan oil fire expert, was called in by the Kuwaiti government to 'solve' the problem. The solution was a complex technique of explosives to remove the oxygen from the flames, thereby putting them out. It was complex, costly and dangerous, and would take many years to complete. Instead, a team of Bulgarians was contracted. Their solution was simple, practical and cost-effective. Using large bulldozers driven by men in fire-resistant suits, they covered the burning oil well heads with sand in a fraction of the time and cost compared to the solution as advocated by Red Adair.

In our logistics business, most staff needed access to computers as the business was dependent on electronic commerce. The business was growing, and the major retailers required their suppliers to trade with them electronically. Growing businesses require cash to keep afloat and the need to purchase dozens of computers for our warehouses was a significant financial burden. Warehouses can be harsh environments for computers which meant they needed replacing regularly. Paying $1,200 for new computers was prohibitive. Considering our problem carefully, we found we didn't need the newest computers with the latest software. The solution was to purchase refurbished computers at less than $200 each, a considerable saving while still being able to do the job.

So, the next time you are *confronted with a problem or the latest technology – stop and think.*

Can the problem be solved simply and cost-effectively, without technology that can often be unnecessarily complicated and expensive?

5.1.3 The lessons from railway tracks

'Most managers were trained to be the thing
they most despise – bureaucrats.'[2]

Alvin Toffler – author and futurist

In Australia, the NSW state railways have the standard railway gauge. This is the distance of 4 feet / 8.5 inches / 1.435 metres between the rails. It is also the gauge used in Great Britain and the US. As an aside, there are two other railway gauges used in Australia, broad and narrow gauge.

The standard gauge is an exceedingly odd number.

Why was that gauge used?

Because that's the railway gauge used in England, and NSW was formerly a British colony.

Why did the British select this gauge?

Because the first railway lines were built by the same people who built the pre-rail tramways. This was the gauge they used.

Why was this gauge used?

Because the engineers who built the tramways used the same jigs that were used for building wagons with the same wheel spacing.

Why did the wagons have this wheel spacing?

Because the wagon wheels used the spacing of the old wheel ruts. Outside these spacings, they would break through the old long-distance roads in England.

So, who built the old rutted roads in England?

Imperial Rome, over 2,000 years ago. Many of these old Roman roads have been used ever since.

And what formed the initial ruts in the roads?

Roman war chariots.

---

2   Attributed to Alvin Toffler, author of best-selling book *"Future Shock"*

Therefore, the NSW standard railway gauge was derived from the original specifications of an Imperial Roman war chariot.

What a great example of the power and life of bureaucracy. *Bureaucracies can live forever.*

When you are handed a specification, procedure or process and fail to understand the 'logic' or 'reason', you can make the statement: *'What horse's arse came up with this?'*

And you may be right. Imperial Roman army chariots were made wide enough to accommodate the rear ends of two war horses.

The moral of the story is to be *'aware of the power and intransigence of bureaucracies'.* This can be outside your organisation or within it.

You need to keep asking the question *'why'* to get the best outcome[3].

5.1.4 Eating a frog

'If it's your job to eat a frog, it's best to do it first thing in the morning. And if it's your job to eat two frogs, it's best to eat the biggest one first.'[4]

Mark Twain – American writer and humourist

When I was growing up in rural Australia, frogs were part of life. Normally they were green tree frogs and could often be found resting inside the overflow of the rainwater tank or in the toilet cistern. As children, we sometimes kept them as pets in a glass tank and fed them insects. However, I was never tempted to eat a green tree frog, although I must admit I have tried frog's legs in a French restaurant.

---

3   See Chapter 4: Processes, section 1: Essentials, part 3: The 5 Whys
4   Attributed to Samuel Clemens, pen name Mark Twain, American writer, humourist, entrepreneur and publisher

How does the metaphor 'eating a frog' relate to productivity?

As managers and business owners, we are confronted each day with tasks and the challenge is to prioritise them. We can create a 'to do list' and then assign importance to each task:

- A – most important
- B – next most important
- C – not important

Determining what is important is a challenge. Managerial tasks can be:

1. **Urgent and important** – crises, deadline-driven activities, customer issues
2. **Not important and urgent** – interruptions such as phone calls and emails, some meetings
3. **Important and not urgent** – strategy and planning, building relationships, major projects
4. **Not important and not urgent** – activities not beneficial to goals, personal emails, internet browsing

One of the major problems for me, personally, and when speaking with other business owners, is that *we do tasks we like doing rather than the tasks we should be doing.* We procrastinate and often avoid the really difficult chores, such as dealing with an employee's performance or visiting a disgruntled customer.

Time is the great equaliser, as you cannot create any more time. Everybody has only 1,440 minutes in a day. The challenge is to manage time to get the best outcomes. The decision-making matrix for time management is a good model to use when determining where your priorities lie and where you should direct your energies to get the best results.

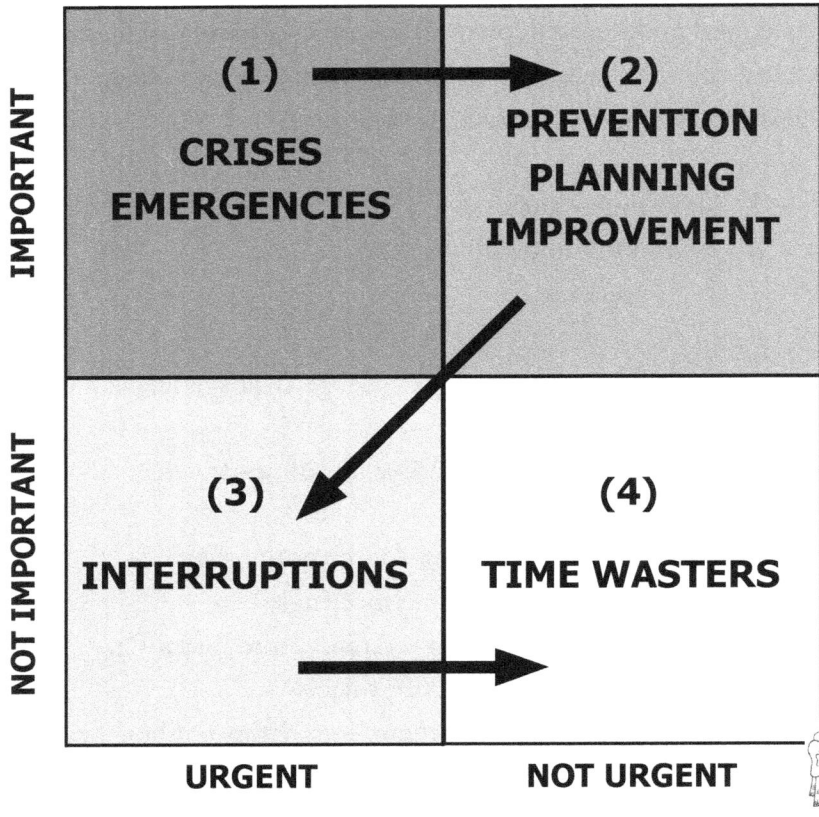

Figure 12: Time Management Priority Matrix

Brian Tracy, in *Eat that Frog!*, outlines some great ways to stop procrastinating and become more productive. Tracy recommends you tackle the most important task first. Likewise, Kevin Kruse, a best-selling *New York Times* author, recommends that you identify your most important task (MIT) and tackle it first thing in your working day in *15 Secrets Successful People Know About Time Management*. Kruse says the most productive hours of the day are first two to three hours where your energy and cognitive ability is at its highest. Your mind is clear and uncluttered by the day's happenings. This tends to be the best time to tackle the task that appears to be the most diffi-cult and insurmountable

By way of comparisons, like Mark Twain, I recommend tackling the hardest task first rather than the most important. That is my frog. While eating your frog may not be the most enjoyable outstanding task, it will energise you to then concentrate on other more impor-tant tasks to be completed during the day. These can be prioritised using the 80/20 rule or Pareto Principle[5]. Having a clear set of goals and a business plan is a good place to start[6].

For example, I needed to advise a sportswear customer that we would be increasing their rates as they no longer reflected the costs of their new order profile, their contract conditions no longer applied and, because of this, we were losing money. I kept putting off see-ing the owner, who was a difficult personality, as I wished to avoid a confrontation, despite this costing the business money. When I finally met the owner, the meeting was less difficult than anticipated and we parted on good terms. Often, when the most difficult task is completed, the rest of the day gets easier and, more importantly, it is not as difficult as first thought. This was certainly the case with the sportswear customer.

How do you manage your time?

Do you have 'to do' lists but don't prioritise your most difficult or important tasks?

What is the best use of your time to achieve your goals and the business' plans, remembering you *only have 1,440 minutes in a day*?

---

5   See Chapter 6: Profits, section 1: Measures, part 2: Focus for success
6   See Chapter 5: Productivity, section 2: Change, part 3: Managerial discipline - are you chasing field mice or antelopes?

5.1.5 Networking

*'The successful networkers I know, the ones receiving
tons of referrals and feeling truly happy about themselves,
continually put the other person's needs ahead of their own.'*[7]
Bob Burg – business book author

A current business buzz word is 'networking'. To be successful in your career or business, networking is considered a vital tool.

So, what is networking, and does it really work?

I once attended a training course where networking was the topic. We were told that the way to network successfully was to attend an event and take 50 business cards with you, then work the room handing out your business card and collecting the other person's card, before moving onto the next person. Your success was gauged by how many business cards you collected. I was horrified at such an approach and argued that this would not work because it was all about what's in it for them and offered nothing to others. I was derided by the presenter.

How would you react to such an approach?

Would the person handing out the cards ever **consider your needs**?

As Bob Burg implies in his quote above, putting other people's needs before yours will make you a more successful networker. Heiner Karst, in *Life Learnings of a Life Coaching*, defines networking as 'the building and maintaining of relationships that lead to opportunities for all parties'. It works with the right attitude and is based on such 'laws' as the law of reciprocity or clichés like **'what goes around, comes around'**.

---

7   Bob Burg, *The Go-Giver: A Little Story about a Powerful Business Idea*, Portfolio, 2007

Here is a great networking example.

I met my friend while undertaking a university course over 25 years ago. We kept in contact and bounced ideas off each other. At one stage, we both worked for the same business and he sparked me to undertake a master's degree. Later, he changed employment leading to the establishment of our logistics business, as his new employer needed outsourced logistics services. The master's degree led me to become a part-time lecturer in postgraduate logistics in Australia and Asia. When my friend relocated to Asia, I visited him on my lecturing trips and he sent some of his staff to the logistics program. When we decided to try and sell our logistics business, he provided a contact that eventually purchased the business. He is now in contact with the business agent who assisted us in selling our business and this is now leading to opportunities for both parties in Asia.

All this was achieved through **maintaining a relationship, looking after other's needs** before your own needs and not burning bridges.

When I started up a new consulting business, there were several people in my consulting network who gave freely of their time and expertise. They put my needs ahead of their own and showed a genuine interest in my business. They have since been 'repaid' as I have been able to engage them to work on some of my business projects – 'what goes around comes around'. Another example is that two of my clients were able to provide recommendations for some house renovations, which benefited their contacts.

Consider **networking as helping others because they, in turn, will help you.**

So, next time you wish to network, what will be your approach?

5.2
CHANGE

5.2.1 What is a KPI?

'The most important performance information that enables organisations or their stakeholders to understand whether the organisation is on track or not.'[8]

Bernard Marr – author and futurist

What is a KPI?

A KPI (Key Performance Indicator) is used to measure the process towards an organisation's goals.

Most managers and business owners know what KPIs are, based on the concept that 'what gets measured gets done'. However, in many instances, *organisations do not know what to measure and this results in poor management, mixed messages and focusing on the wrong things*. One mistake is to confuse KPIs with goals. The goal of a business may be to increase sales to $20 million, however, this is not a KPI.

One of our first customers in our logistics business was a major Australian retailer who built a new store in a major shopping centre. Retailers normally have a KPI which measures sales per metre of their retail area. The 'whiz kids' at the retailer's head office decided to minimise the 'in-store' storage areas to increase the total sales area.

Within weeks of opening the new store, sales were suffering. The stock could not be replenished from the back of the store because not enough stock could be stored there. This resulted in reduced staff morale and a new requirement to operate an off-site warehouse to replenish the store daily, which increased costs considerably. This is an example of a poor implementation of a KPI. The challenge is to select the right KPIs.

Why are KPIs important?

KPIs, if structured correctly as measuring activities towards a business's goals, can have a positive impact on performance at all levels of a business. For example, KPIs can empower staff by showing them how they can make a difference to the business, as well as holding them accountable.

In our logistics business, we designed a system that collected productivity data by customer, job and product category. The warehouses were divided into sections, each headed by a supervisor responsible for the customers and staff in their section. Each week, we produced productivity data by job and customer which we called 'the marking rate'. This information was shared with the supervisor, empowering them to make a difference to the business, by holding them accountable, involving their team and demonstrating how important their team was in the business. *They were empowered, which increased their levels of job satisfaction immeasurably.* The marking rate was a measure which drove the business's profits.

Not only do some organisations have the wrong KPIs, they often have too many KPIs. In my experience, the number of KPIs should be restricted to between three and five, otherwise they can become too hard to measure and manage. I have seen large companies with literally dozens of KPIs, which rarely relate to the company's goals. The challenge is to identify the key indicators that help the business succeed.

What are the **three main considerations** in setting KPIs?

1. *Ensure they are simple, easily measurable and understood.*
    For example, in long-distance road transport, KPIs
    could be revenue per kilometre, kilometre per vehicle
    and fuel cost per kilometre. These performance indicators
    are easily understood and measurable.
2. *The measures must be key indicators of performance
    and directly linked to strategy.*
    Using road transport, the strategy is to maximise
    both kilometres travelled and revenue, so measuring
    revenue per kilometre is sensible.
3. *Minimise the number of KPIs, thereby making them
    relevant to all.*
    KPIs can be more precisely developed by using
    Key Performance Questions (KPQ), which assist
    in objectively developing activity measures that lead
    towards meeting the business' goals. Here are some
    examples:
    *   What are the activities we should measure
        that lead to high customer retention?
    *   What should we measure that indicates
        profitability by customer?
    *   Are the current productivity measures linked
        to the business' goals?

5.2.2 Management by walking around

*'The simple act of paying positive attention to people
has a great deal to do with productivity.'*[9]

Tom Peters – American business writer

I was recently discussing with a friend how the first six months of
their new job was going. It was a role which required both senior
management experience and technical expertise and was critical to
the organisation and its members. The friend was quite happy with
their new role. They had autonomy and were able to work on projects unhindered. However, they were puzzled that, in the head office
of about 60 people, they had never seen the CEO. That's right – not
even physically sighted the CEO, let alone met them.

This seems like an extraordinary situation, but it's true. It would
hardly come as a surprise that, in the previous 12-month period, over
30 new people were employed to replace those who had left. It can
be safely assumed that there was something seriously wrong with this
organisation. In this case, the statement **'a fish goes rotten at the head
first'**, explaining organisational failure would appear to be true.

Staff look for leadership, not aloofness. Evidence clearly indicates
that successful organisations have management teams that are
engaged with their customers and staff. One demonstration of this is
the concept of 'management by walking around'. This is not a 'royal
tour', as experienced in one of my first jobs as a fresh-faced junior. At
that time, I worked for a large multinational in the steel industry and
whenever senior executives were about to tour, there was a frenzy of
painting and clean up – much to the bemusement of staff. The tour
was generally a five-minute walk-through, accompanied by the plant

---

9   Attributed to Tom Peters, author of *In Search of Excellence*

manager, before the entourage moved on to the next plant. Little wonder that the business had to merge later and divest its manufacturing to remain in business.

Early on in my career, I developed the practice of **'walking the floor'** within an hour of arriving at work to talk to staff. It was amazing what an effect it had on morale. Problems were aired and often solved, giving staff a sense of satisfaction. It was also another way of providing feedback on performance and hearing about issues with customers and suppliers. People like nothing better than being asked for their opinions in a considered and professional manner.

My suggestion is that if you are *not* managing by walking around, plan to start this as soon as you can. It will work wonders, make your job easier, help with workforce engagement and increase profits. In *Sam Walton: Made in America,* Sam Walton, the founder of Walmart, names one of his six strategies for success as 'keep your ear to the ground and go into the store'.

However, ensure that you are genuine in your approach. Your workforce will pick up fake concern and self-serving behaviour immediately. I can recall another CEO in a much smaller organisation who would stroll through the workplace, stopping and asking a plant operator the name of the person who they were to next meet. They would then walk up to that person and say, 'Hello, Mary' as if they were some long-lost friend, but not engaging in any meaningful dialogue before rushing off to the next person. You can imagine how he was viewed by staff. It later became a game to give him the wrong name and see what the reaction was.

Are you managing by walking around?

If not, when will you start?

Management by walking around makes great sense and makes for a better workplace, providing it is done sincerely, in a considered and professional manner.

5.2.3 Managerial discipline - are you chasing field mice or antelopes?

'A lion is fully capable of capturing, killing, and eating a field mouse. But it turns out that the energy required to do so exceeds the caloric content of the mouse itself. So, a lion that spent its day hunting and eating field mice would slowly starve to death. A lion can't live on field mice. A lion needs antelope. Antelope are big animals. They take more speed and strength to capture and kill, and once killed, they provide a feast for the lion and her pride ... So, ask yourself at the end of the day, 'Did I spend today chasing mice or hunting antelope?'[10]

Newt Gingrich – speaker of the US House of Representatives

What is Gingrich's underlying message?

Certainly, the Pareto Principle, or 80/20 rule, is implied in this quotation[11]. However, there is another message for managers and business owners here: to focus with discipline on the issues that provide the best return for your resources of time, money and expertise. The danger is business failure, as explained by Michael E Gerber in *The e-Myth Revisited – Why Most Small Businesses Don't Work and What to Do About It*. This is where a business owner and manager who understands the technical nature of the business but does not understand the business, is likely to fail. In summary, they do what they are comfortable in doing and what they know, not what they should be doing.

Jim Collins, in *Good to Great*, describes how a 'culture of discipline' is evident in successful companies. This begins with disciplined

---

10   Attributed to Newt Gingrich, US Politician although originally it is an African fable
11   See Chapter 6: Profits, section 1: Measures, part 2: Focus for success

leaders who display empathy, personal humility and intense focus. They do not suffer from 'I' strain[12] and rarely appear in the media, seeking celebrity. Before purchasing our logistics business, I worked for a privately-owned transport company. In an industry known for its larger-than-life personalities who courted the media, the owner was virtually unknown. He ran a highly successful business, which was far more profitable than many of the publicly listed companies in the industry. He was extremely disciplined in strictly adhering to his market niche, which enabled higher profits and greater customer service.

In another example of discipline, I managed a large division of a transport business in a large regional centre, where the managing director was passionate about truck safety. This involved vehicle journeys being monitored by onboard computers to prevent speeding, exceeding mandated driving hours and excessive idling which wastes fuel. If drivers exceeded the speed limit by 5% in a week, they were disciplined. If this occurred three times within 12 months, the driver was terminated. Like the lion, it was targeting the areas that significantly affected the successful operation of the business. Each week, the performance of the trucks and drivers was given to me to action. I decided, against the advice of my peers, to post the results on the drivers' notice board.

Did the drivers react negatively to being compared to others, as I had been warned would occur?

No.

Instead, each week, many of the drivers would compare the performance of their vehicles and themselves. Some drivers would personally seek me out to ask if there were problems with their vehicle and why, for example, their vehicle had appeared to be idling

---

excessively. They became self-disciplined team members who were more accountable and didn't need to be micromanaged. Fuel economy improved and, more importantly, our accident record was the best in the business, despite having the drivers who travelled the most kilometres each week company-wide. Within the 'safety framework', a culture of freedom and responsibility had developed.

For a business to grow or change in a positive way, discipline is required where consistent behaviours align with achieving the organisation's goals. Note the words – 'discipline' and 'consistent'. The aim is for consistent, productive, goal-oriented behaviours to become habits. **Habits, once formed, become entrenched – however, they must be the right habits and they must align with the organisation's vision and goals.** In the drivers' example, safety and performance became a habit. With the niche transport company, the discipline was remaining in its narrow market niche only. Both examples required disciplined people acting in a disciplined manner, demonstrating that discipline must start at the top.

Here is another example. I was engaged to undertake a business review by a niche logistics business which had suddenly begun losing money. Determining the prime reason was relatively easy. The business had lost a major customer who had contributed the most to their previous profits. However, this was only a symptom of what was wrong. A walk-through their numerous warehouses provided some answers. The warehouses were dirty, the stock was not in the correct locations and the staff were inadequately supervised. Management was focussed on managing the day-to-day crises and were not enforcing operational disciplines, rates had not increased in several years and customer service was inconsistent. Classic 'chasing field mice' behaviour.

The business review formed the basis of a new business plan[13]. Benchmarks for performance were established and a renewed commitment to improving customer service was implemented. This was underpinned by imposing operational disciplines in the warehouse, following consultative meetings with staff. Several managers and supervisors exited the business, and a new general manager and senior management team were appointed. In the first year, the company made a modest profit. In the second year, profits exceeded expectations, revenue grew through targeted strategic sales in the business's market niche, prices increased, unprofitable customers were forced from the businesses, a warehouse was closed and new leases with more favourable terms were negotiated. This was a good, practical example of what Jim Collins describes in *Good to Great – disciplined people, disciplined thought, confronting the brutal facts, and disciplined action. A culture of discipline.*

Being a successful business owner, leader and manager requires discipline. **Lack of discipline manifests itself physically**[14] in examples such as untidy and dirty warehouses, poor telephone manners and uninspiring first impressions.

What are the antelopes you should be hunting in your organisation?

Have you identified the field mice?

Is it clear to others in the business?

Do the antelopes align with your vision, values and goals?

Discipline in the areas of accountability, teamwork, and attention to detail are required. *Disciplined leadership is defined by sound habits, rigour, consistency and routines.* A disciplined environment assists in

---

13   See Chapter 3: Planning, section 2: Roadmap, part 2: Business plan – why the journey is more important than the destination?

14   See Chapter 5: Productivity, section 3: Consistency, part 5: Recognising poorly managed organisations

putting both management and employees on their best behaviour, leading to improved productivity and profits.

5.2.4 What can Elvis teach us about business?

'I'm as helpless as can be
I become a puppet on a string'
From Elvis Presley's song 'Puppet on a String'

It is over 40 years since the death of the 'King of Rock-n-Roll', Elvis Presley.

What has this got to do with business?
Elvis died of a heart attack at the relatively young age of 42. Exemplified by his estate at Graceland in Memphis, Elvis became known for a life of excess and luxury, owning three pink Cadillacs and a private jet. This lifestyle finally caught up with him. Years of substance abuse and poor dietary habits resulted in multiple ailments including glaucoma, high blood pressure, liver damage and an enlarged colon. He went from a sex symbol to an overweight, unhealthy, almost bankrupt man who died a premature death.

It is a sad story of decline through excess and poor choices and could parallel a business failing for similar reasons. For example, Kodak grew fat on a film-based processing business model and, despite inventing the digital camera, filed for bankruptcy in 2012. However, there is another, more **positive lesson** from the Elvis Presley story.

When Elvis died in 1977, he had less than USD $1 million in his bank account and probably would have been bankrupt within a few years, had he lived. However, in 2016, his estate earned more than USD $27 million, with total sales heading towards USD $1.5 billion.

What is the lesson or message here?

Businesses must be able to continue to prosper and grow without the owner or CEO having to work in the business. Like the words of the Elvis song *'Puppet On a String'*, businesses should not be solely reliant on the owner or CEO.

The Elvis Presley 'business' (his estate) continued to grow significantly after his death.

What is the takeaway message of what I call the **Elvis Business Model (EBM)?**

Have a business that can operate without you working in the business on a day-to-day basis. In other words, have a business continuity plan[15].

What are you, as a business owner or manager doing about creating a business that can operate without you daily?

5.2.5 Lessons from a master rugby coach

'There are people who lead and lead inspirationally, and those who don't.'

Eddie Jones – English rugby coach

In 2017, the England national rugby team had won 18 test matches without a loss, having won the 2016 Six Nations Championship and with a three-nil win against the Wallabies in Australia. Previously, England had only won three tests there in 100 years[16].

What has brought about this amazing run of wins?

---

15   See Chapter 3: Planning, section 2: Roadmap

16   Post script: England lost to Ireland in their 19th game, 13-9, denying them a world record.

The English team was coached by Eddie Jones, a former coach of the Wallabies. In 2015, as the coach of the Japanese side, he orchestrated one of the greatest upsets in the history of the sport with Japan defeating the South African Springboks in the Rugby World Cup.

Japanese culture is very different from that of England. Jones had to adjust his style of coaching to match the culture. In Japan, as head coach, everyone does as you say. With the old **'command and control'** style of management, there was no room for initiative and self-reliance.

It was different, however, when Jones took up the position of England's coach. Former Wallaby coach Bob Dwyer described Jones as follows:

'He calls a spade a shovel, Eddie. I consider myself a very direct Australian, but Eddie is more so than I am. He takes no prisoners at all.'[17]

While being a strict disciplinarian and setting clear expectations for performance, Jones adopted a different approach to the one he used when coaching Japan. He created an environment where players were **allowed to make decisions.**

'You can't develop leadership qualities if you don't allow players to make decisions. You can't develop leadership qualities if you don't allow people to make mistakes. It is a very difficult balance, but you have to allow it,' says Jones[18].

'You need players who have leadership qualities to make decisions for themselves'.

---

17   https://www.theaustralian.com.au/weekend-australian-magazine/how-eddie-jones-transformed-english-rugby/news-story
18   IBID

Jones is a former teacher and headmaster. Perhaps his experience here helped in his coaching.

Jones has demonstrated some of the real characteristics of a leader – developing people, generating enthusiasm, inspiring trust, motivating, challenging the status quo[19] and modifying your leadership approach to match the circumstances.

Can you think of a circumstance where you were allowed to make decisions and this process **developed you as a leader?**

Have you **developed others** as leaders by allowing them **to make decisions?**

---

19   See Chapter 1: People, section 1: Leadership

5.3
CONSISTENCY

5.3.1 The importance of standard routines and procedures

'Routine sets you free.'[20]

Verne Harnish – founder of Young Entrepreneurs' Organization (YEO)

One of the biggest issues faced by businesses as they grow is managing the growth. This is because their *management systems come under strain.*

Many businesses begin when a **'technician'** for example, a tradesman such as an electrician, decides that they want to go into business as they have the *technical expertise.* The new entrepreneur thinks that *because they understand the technical work, they also understand how the business operates.*

This is a myth, according to author Michael Gerber. In his book, published over 30 years ago, *The E-Myth Revisited*, Gerber introduced the concept that very successful businesses have *very simple and robust business systems* that do not require exceptional managers. The more automatic and simplified your management system, the more effective your business. What Gerber is explaining is a franchise system.

Very early in my corporate career, I worked for a company called **Pioneer Concrete International**. The company grew from a single pre-mixed concrete plant in Sydney in the early 1950s to a major

---

20 Verne Harnish, *Scaling Up: How a Few Companies Make It..and why the Rest Don't*, Gezelles, 2014

industrial corporation operating in 11 countries within 30 years. The founder was an accountant called Sir Tristan Antico and he was obviously not a concrete 'technician'. The primary foundation of the pre-mixed concrete business was a concept called **'cell management'**, where the plant manager was responsible for marketing, production, human resources, sales, quality and profitability. As a young graduate, it was an exciting and challenging work environment, where you quickly learnt business management skills, or left.

Antico designed a very *simple management system*. Remember, this was before computers. Each fortnight, the manager reported their profit and loss using standard forms, showing gross margins, sales and profits. Material purchases and usage were reconciled monthly. The company could tell very quickly how it was travelling using this **standardised and disciplined system** – regionally, nationally and internationally. What I learnt at Pioneer, I carried on to other companies I worked for and then to our own business.

As Vern Harnish says in *Scaling Up: How a Few Companies Make It...and Why the Rest Don't;* 'Routine sets you free'.

This *disciplined, routine and systematic management system* allowed Pioneer to expand quickly into international markets well before other competitors. Their business system was **scaleable** without the administrative and management bottlenecks often encountered when companies grow. One of my former managers said a trained monkey could run the Pioneer Concrete system.

As Warren Buffett, the great American investor said:

'Buy into a business that's doing so well an idiot could run it, because sooner or later, one will.'[21]

This was one of the main keys to Pioneer's success. Interestingly, a new CEO recruited from outside the organisation had no allegiance

---

21   Associated Press, 20 May 2008 story on Warren Buffett

to the system. The cell management system, with its *standardised and disciplined management system*, was abandoned. The business was subsequently acquired by a major international competitor and an Australian industrial icon was lost.

The questions for any business owner are:

Are **your business systems scaleable** so that your company can manage its growth without losing control?

Will they allow you to work on the business rather in it?'

5.3.2 Beware the hero manager...

'Effective leadership is putting first things first.
Effective management is discipline in carrying it out.'[22]
   Stephen R Covey – author and businessman

Did you hear about the transport operations manager who worked all night to get the freight loaded on the trucks and out on time? Or the warehouse manager who worked all weekend to relocate stock in the warehouse to make it more efficient?

If you were running these companies, what would you do?

1. Recognise them in the company newsletter?
2. Promote them?
3. Reprimand them?

As managers and business owners, most of us would probably choose (1) or (2), wouldn't we?

But is it really the right thing to do?

---

22   Steven R Covey, *The Seven Habits of Highly Effective People*, Free Press, 1989

I worked for a major transport company many years ago. The company was characterised by a 'can do' culture where anything would be done to get the load out. We worked long hours for at least six days per week. The operations managers, like the examples here, were treated as heroes. They embodied the values prized by the organisation – toughness, persistence, and long hours at work. These managers were celebrated and promoted.

However, when you probed the situations in greater depth, it was clear that the *real underlying problem was that these management heroes had not been doing a good job of managing their day-to-day activities – in particular, planning and training*. In other words, the more mundane tasks were often not recognised. If these tasks had been done, the crisis would have been prevented. However, by celebrating the 'heroic' actions, the company's top management was telling the organisation that it was okay to not do the quiet, unobserved day-to-day work if they responded forcefully to the problems that inevitably resulted. The quiet achievers were not recognised, nor rewarded.

The message was: **crisis response is more important than crisis prevention.**

The transport company was subsequently taken over, as it struggled to provide the required returns to its shareholders. Top management left. Subsequently, a new management team was installed that reorganised operations. The new senior managers understood the importance of crisis prevention and developed a new focus on planning, both daily and in the long term. One of the biggest problems was that the middle and upper-middle managers in place had been promoted for managing a crisis, not for their management skills. They were not skilled in crisis prevention and, importantly, their personalities were more suited to the action-oriented crisis response than the more systematic and analytical process of crisis prevention. They soon followed senior management out of the company.

We also see this in sales. When a major customer has a problem, the alarm sounds, and everyone rushes to fix the problem. The sales manager is celebrated as a hero, as they have saved the account and maintained the relationship. Picture the leader on a white stallion, leading his troops in a cavalry charge – noise, action and recognition. In contrast, the sales reps who are skilled at maintaining and slowly growing major accounts often remain in the shadows, unappreciated and unrecognised.

In good companies, sales leaders understand the process of quiet, steady account development. This involves mapping a customer's buying process, understanding how to increase a customer's profitability, and seamlessly involving operations managers with their customer counterparts to reduce the costs for both customer and supplier. This is a long process, but it creates customer relationships with high sustainability, profitability and growth.

The first question is: Who is the real sales hero?

The second question is: Are the managers, the ones who quietly drive major sales increases and cost reductions, the real operations heroes?

In my experience, most of these 'heroes' are skilled at managing a crisis that was avoidable. Often, their companies were suffering problems that should not have occurred in the first place, due to poor management and systems. The real heroes in an organisation are those managers who have the wisdom and insight to develop systematic information, processes, and behavioural drivers, which enable their managers and staff to coordinate their activities to achieve more together. The result is that their management teams form effective coordinated processes and develop a culture of profitability. **Effective leaders are not those on the white charger but the opposite. They are not dramatic, romantic, heroic or exciting – just very effective**[23].

---

23   See Chapter 5: Productivity, section 3: Consistency, part 5: Recognising poorly managed organisations

Like teaching, one of the truisms of management is that you get what you expect. If you celebrate the mythical operations and sales heroes, you will get mediocre performance and continual crises punctuated by occasional 'heroic' displays. *A good manager must have the foresight to systematically create the conditions that enable their managers to improve performance and prevent crises, thus creating a great business.*

As a manager, you have a choice…

5.3.3 Procrastination and egos cost businesses.

'It does not take much strength to do things, but it requires a great deal of strength to decide what to do.'[24]

Elbert Hubbard – writer, publisher and philosopher

How often, as business owners and managers, do we *procrastinate* making decisions because of the feared consequences?

Sometimes we put off making the most obvious decisions and further compound indecision by allowing **our egos to rule**, rather than **practical common sense**.

Let me give you an example.

Recently, a client was caught up in a situation that not only cost the business significant money but was a major distraction for the business in general. An employee who was still within their probationary period was responsible for bullying two other employees, causing them to leave. Despite my advice that the offender should be terminated without recourse, as they were within their probationary period, the owner procrastinated, and the offending employee remained employed after their probationary period. The owner then decided to act on the advice and terminate the employee, who

---

24   Attributed to Elbert Hubbard, writer, publisher and philosopher

immediately filed for 'unfair dismissal'. Australia's employment laws make it quite difficult to terminate employees after their probationary period and court-imposed penalties are high.

I advised the owner to make a one-off payment to make the problem 'go away'. He refused, stating it was against his principles to make such a payment. Lawyers were engaged, time was spent to present the case to the government tribunal, and everybody was distracted. *The indirect cost was considerable.* The offender then doubled their demand for 'go away' money. The final outcome was a large legal bill plus a payout to the 'offender' and wasted time and effort by the business owner and the legal advisors.

All this was avoidable. The offender should have been terminated within their probation period[25]. Their actions had already resulted in two long-term employees leaving the business. This was poor management. The second piece of advice, to pay out the claim would have also solved the problem. However, **pride and ego ruled the roost, rather than common sense**.

In business, sometimes we must **put our pride and ego aside** and **make a decision that is best for the business.** I have been guilty of this in my career. However, several painful experiences have caused me to reflect on my actions.

Can you think of an example where you *procrastinated* or *allowed your ego to delay making a decision?*

Did you *discard common sense advice* and make the **wrong decision**?

What did you learn from this experience?

---

25   See Chapter 2: People, section 3: Teamwork

5.3.4 It didn't happen if it's not written down

'If it is not written down, it does not exist.'[26]

Philippe Kruchten – Academic and software engineer

If it is not written down, it didn't happen. Now that's a big statement.

Does this sound absurd?

Is it the truth?

Many years ago, I was listening to a recording of oral family history. It was claimed by a distant cousin that her father (my great grandfather) met the bushranger Thunderbolt (bushrangers were outlaws and highwaymen) when he was a young boy. Thunderbolt arrived unexpectedly early one morning on his father's small land holding in the New England district of New South Wales. The story goes that Thunderbolt joined them for breakfast and, while having breakfast, he kept looking nervously out the window. Thanking them for their hospitality, he gave them a gold sovereign, mounted his horse and rode off. Not long afterward, some mounted police arrived. Apparently, this occurred in 1864. When I checked the dates, I found that my great grandfather was not born until 1866 and Thunderbolt was in jail in 1864. Although the event probably happened, it did not happen in 1864.

There is a business lesson here. Written records should not be underestimated. Don't rely on memory.

My advice is to *write down* and *record the most important things*.

If a legal issue arises, the written word is far more reliable than someone's recollection. It is important, particularly with issues of people management and workplace health and safety.

Let me give you an example.

---

26 Attributed to Phillippe Kruchten, Canadian Professor of Software Engineering

As a young manager in my mid-20s, I was managing a concrete plant in Canberra. The fleet of owner-drivers continuously threatened and intimidated me. It was an unusual situation when looked at through today's eyes. The drivers were independent businessmen who owned concrete trucks. This was the same for other ready-mix concrete companies also operating in Canberra. Despite being businessmen, the owner-drivers were all members of a trade union. With the union's assistance, they restricted the number of trucks operating, thereby restricting competition and increasing the rates they could charge.

It was a business cartel which was restricting competition. It was not a legal or government-sanctioned cartel, such as taxi plate licenses. The construction industry was booming and the capacity to deliver concrete was restricted, adversely affecting the industry. The situation deteriorated to a point where the driver's representative in our business tried to tell us when and to whom we could deliver concrete.

This was clearly illegal under the Trade Practices Act. Businesses are not allowed to collude in order to restrict competition and increase prices. This 'arrangement' was adversely affecting our customers. On several occasions, I was confronted and threatened. Having some knowledge of the law and knowing that this 'arrangement' was probably illegal, when threatened I quoted back that what they were doing was illegal. *I then noted it in my work diary.*

More than three years after I had left the business, I received a call from the company's lawyer. The new CEO had decided to use Canberra as a test case to initially overturn the 'arrangements' and then use it as a precedent in the state of New South Wales, to break up the arrangements there. Luckily, I had kept my work diaries and, when called as a court witness, was able to quote the times, dates and conversations. The company won the court case and the cartel arrangement that had been supported by the union was quashed.

This outcome demonstrates the importance of recording events, as the diary entries were one of the main reasons the court case was won. Too often in business, we are busy and fail to record important events, only to find out later that they should have been. The ready-mix drivers' case was an important learning experience for me.

Employee issues such as performance management and safety requirements are important areas, where discussions and events must be recorded. *Our memories cannot be relied upon, as we cannot remember dates, times and actual conversations offhand.*

The Thunderbolt story illustrates the *unreliability of oral history and memory.* As managers, writing down important things is not optional. Many of us hate paperwork, however it is an essential part of our job.

What should you, as a manager, **be recording**?

Where should you **file these records**?

5.3.5 Recognising poorly managed organisations

'Unfortunately, it's also true to say that good management is a bit like oxygen – it's invisible and you don't notice its presence until it's gone, and then you're sorry.'[27]

Charles Stross – British science fiction writer

Have you ever walked into a business and realised it was poorly managed before you have even met the management team?

Years of experience has sharpened my 'antennae' to organisations with poor management. The symptoms are apparent even when you first come into contact with the business or organisation.

---

27   Charles Stross, *The Fuller Memorandum*, Mass Market Paperback, 2011

Think about the last time you visited an organisation. *What were your first impressions?* They are generally a guide to the rest of the business. A recent visit to a company proved that my first impressions were correct. The reception was untidy and dirty. There was no visitors' book, no induction procedure and no chair to sit on while waiting for the owner. No coffee, tea or water was offered at the meeting. The meeting room where customers would obviously meet staff had broken chairs with paper and cardboard boxes on the board table. When I politely requested a cup of coffee, there were no clean coffee mugs or milk.

Was this initial experience an indication of how the business was managed?

Yes, of course it was.

The staff were surly and demotivated, and initiative was discouraged. The owner treated them poorly, exacerbated by his erratic behaviour. The business went into administration within four months of my visit.

By comparison, another business I visited was the opposite. Although the office area was 'dated', it was neat and tidy. A drink was offered and there were pictures on the wall showing what the company did, together with certificates of appreciation from charities. The company's values were prominently displayed. I subsequently found out that this company was growing profitably at 20% per annum and had been doing so for the past three years.

Another indicator is telephone manner. For example, if the phone is not answered promptly, if the person does not state the company name or introduce themselves, and does not have a helpful and pleasant manner, then it is probably a symptom of poor management. Telephones are the face of the business and often the first point of interaction with customers.

As an extension of this theory, **we often don't notice good managers or good customers until they have left.** They are often 'invisible' and do their job without 'noise'[28].

Good management is like a well-serviced motor vehicle that performs well and does not break down.

Good managers recognise this in their staff, customers and suppliers…do you?

---

28   See Chapter 5: Productivity, section 3: Consistency, part 2: Beware the hero manager

6
PROFITS

The last or fifth 'P' is profit. The elephant has been cooked successfully. The inedible parts have been sold, the ivory has been treasured (because it's illegal to sell ivory), and the hide has been tanned and made into leather goods. We have made money from the sale of the leather.

What are the measures of success in finally eating the elephant?

What about the meat we can't eat? Can we sell it?

Should we put aside some meat and preserve it?

Do we celebrate the success by having a feast?

Was the exercise worthwhile? Was it profitable? Would we do it again?

6.1
Measures

6.1.1 Exit strategy...

'You only get one Alan Bond in your life time, and I've had mine.'[1]

Kerry Packer – billionaire Australian media owner

The late Kerry Packer sold his TV business to corporate raider Alan Bond for over $1 billion in 1987 – far more than it was worth – and then bought it back three years later for $250 million. He was not expecting the sale, but he sold because it was too good an offer to refuse.

'Begin with the end in mind.' This is habit two in Stephen Covey's *The Seven Habits of Highly Effective People,* and it is important when you start or buy into a business.

What is your end game?

What do you want to achieve and where do you want to be in X years' time?

I bought into a business nearly 20 years ago with three other partners. In purchasing the business, the seller who was our former employer, advised us to have an exit strategy with a time limit. This was noted and promptly forgotten.

As the business grew, there were the usual tragedies and triumphs. After 10 years, I suggested we needed to get the business in a 'sale

---

1   As quoted by *The Sydney Morning Herald,* 28 December 2005

ready' condition. However, with business partners with differing priorities, this did not eventuate. It's not that we needed or wanted to sell the business. It was as the late Kerry Packer said, 'You never know when a buyer will come along.'

Without warning, a potential buyer did come along, and we were not ready. It was a disaster. The potential purchaser viewed a somewhat disorganised business and quickly lost interest. An underlying issue was the lack of a shared vision within the management team and unclear agendas.

Did we learn anything from our first approach by a potential buyer? A little bit, but not enough…

Less than two years later, we were approached by a large multinational company wanting to buy the business. This time, we were a little better prepared. The negotiations dragged on for over nine months and eventually failed, for several reasons. They included legal complexities to do with selling the business versus selling the company with its significant negative financial implications, the final offer, and performance guarantees.

I was disappointed that we had missed another opportunity. At our debriefing meeting, I identified what I believed were the reasons for the sale falling through:

1. No professional assistance from a corporate advisor – the potential purchaser had an entire mergers and acquisitions (M&A) department
2. No legal or tax advice
3. No timeline

There were, however, some positives that came out of this experience. The business had now been 'tidied up' and was in a more saleable position. After considerable discussion, it was then agreed to engage an advisor, seek financial and tax advice, and agree on a timeline should a buyer emerge.

The engagement of the corporate advisor was critical[2]. They helped take the emotion out of the process, kept to the plan, prepared professional sale documentation, coordinated the various parties including the accountant and lawyers, and sought out potential buyers. The corporate advisor uncovered and highlighted the value drivers of the business. The business was sold successfully to an offshore company at a price that far exceeded our expectations.

Our Alan Bond moment.

In hindsight, perhaps the failed sales helped us. You can be lucky and learn from your mistakes.

Is your business ready for sale just in case an Alan Bond comes along with an offer too good to refuse?

Are you mentally and emotionally ready to sell your business?

6.1.2 Focus for success

'If you're Noah, and your ark is about to sink, look for the elephants first, because you can throw over a bunch of cats, dogs, squirrels, and everything else that is just a small animal and your ark will keep sinking. But if you can find one elephant to get overboard, you're in much better shape.'[3]

Vilfredo Pareto - Italian engineer, sociologist, economist and philosopher

Today we hear people say, 'things are not what they used to be' and 'years ago, there were more opportunities'.

Do you really think this is the case?

---

2   See Chapter 3: Planning, section 1: Framework, part 5: What are the foundations of a good business?

3   Attributed to Italian economist Vilfredo Pareto whose research led to the 80/20 rule.

In my experience, the real issue is that today we face *too many opportunities* and we have *too little focus.* We get busier and busier and seem to achieve less and less – fighting bushfires rather than preventing them in the first place.

The reasons for this are many.

Often, we focus on things we enjoy doing rather than what we *should be* doing. We are in our comfort zone. For example, a manager meets with the people they like or get on with, avoiding those who are difficult or are problematic. A salesperson calls on those clients and prospective clients who are close by or are easy to deal with. We are all guilty of doing this.

Have you heard of the **Pareto Principle**? This is often called the **80/20 rule**:

- 80% of sales come from 20% of our customers
- 20% of our customers give us 80% of our problems
- 20% of our customers demand 80% of our valuable time
- 80% of sales come from 20% of our products.

Time, expertise and money are limited resources.

Therefore, it is important to try and apply the Pareto Principle in our business and work-life to get the best return. Before going into business, I worked for a logistics company with an identified market niche in which they specialised. They were extremely focussed on staying in this niche and were not tempted to expand outside it. The company had less than six customers, profitability was far above the industry average and it was eventually sold for an exceptional profit.

What was the lesson?

It is obvious.

Identify the areas that give you the greatest return for your time and resources and do not be distracted by other issues. *Focus* on what is important and not on what you like doing. This requires *discipline* and is more easily said than done.

Here are some practical applications:

- To reduce costs, identify which 20% of your customers are using 80% of the resources. With those who are not top profit generators, charge them for the resources they consume.
- To maximise personal productivity, realise that 80% of your time is spent on trivial activities. Analyse and identify which activities produce the most value to your company. Then focus and concentrate on the vital few (20%). With the 'leftovers', delegate or discontinue doing them.
- To increase profits, focus your attention on the vital few customers (top 20%). Identify and rank your customers in order of profits. Then focus your sales activities on them. The 80/20 rule predicts that 20% of the customers generate 80% of the revenues, and 20% yield 80% of the profits, however these two groups are not necessarily the same 20%.

If you wish to use the Pareto Principle to your advantage, the first step is to get started. Put your ideas down on paper. Do not think too hard, as you may become distracted. Once down on paper, you can then work through your list and prioritise. A great tool that helps with decision-making is the Four Segments diagram in Figure 13.

Achieve

- Is it required or necessary?
- If YES, then achieve it.

Preserve

- Do you have it or need it?
- If YES, then preserve it.

Action Matrix

Avoid

- Is it required?
- If NO, then avoid it.

Eliminate

- Do you have it and don't require it?
- If YES, then eliminate it.

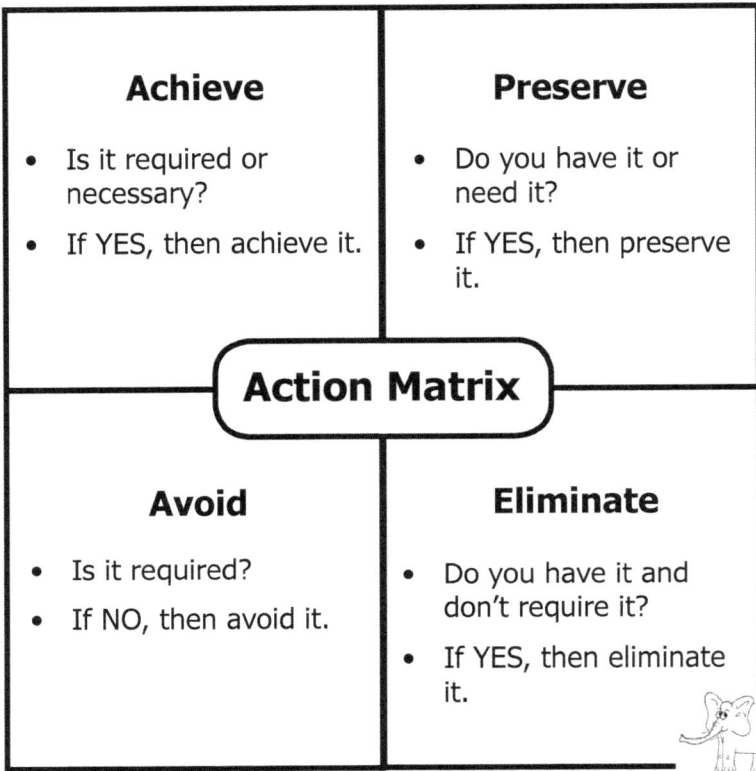

Figure 13: Decision Making Matrix

Here is a simple exercise that will help you prioritise your time and maximise outcomes. On a sheet of paper, draw up three columns with the following headings:

1. *Things only you can do* – this should focus on your strengths and be critical to the business's success
2. *Things you hate doing* – these tasks are probably those that you put off, and there are likely to be people in the business who are better at these tasks
3. *Things you should not be doing* – what is the best use of your time? Are you doing things that are not key to the

business's success? Would we be more effective managers if we created **'Stop Doing Lists'?** Jim Collins, author of *Good to Great*, certainly thinks so.

In conclusion, too often we spend time on creating to do lists and not prioritising.

Where is your *energy best directed to maximise outcomes?*

6.1.3 What are the three major mistakes business owners make with financial reporting?

'Stay on top of your finances. Don't leave that up to others.'[4]
Leif Garrett – US singer and TV personality

I meet many business owners who tell me that their external accountants do their monthly accounts. In fact, one owner had his external accountant and his bookkeeper on site each week, and another waited three months to get his monthly profit and loss statement (P&L) – which he didn't look at anyway.

Did they provide financial reports that helped these owners manage their businesses?

This depends on the *type of reports* being created.

However, the answer is almost always… **NO**.

What is usually provided is a service to input financial data and/or accounting services required for taxation purposes, that is to meet compliance requirements. The owners would then be given a P&L statement, with total revenue less all the costs consolidated under the heading of 'costs' to calculate either a profit or a loss. The costs are not separated into the types of costs; fixed, variable and overheads.

---

4   Attributed to Leif Garrett, US Singer and TV personality

Why is this a problem?

This is a problem because these P&Ls are not *operational* P&Ls. This brings me to one of my favourite issues with managing businesses. The financial results that are being currently reported do not help in operating the business[5].

In my experience, there are *three mistakes* business owners make in financial reporting:

1. *Incorrectly categorised costs*
    Many businesses do not understand the difference between fixed, variable and overhead costs. Furthermore, external accountants generally do not categorise those costs, as this is not required for compliance or taxation purposes. For example, it is important to know what your direct or variable costs are, as they vary with output or sales revenue. By not categorising costs correctly and having them in the correct section of the accounts, you cannot determine your gross margin, sometimes called your gross profit which is the revenue minus the direct or variable costs (or COGS – cost of goods sold)

2. *Reports do not reflect operational needs*
    When costs and revenue are not put in the correct place, they will not help operationally. By consolidating costs, rather than categorising them, a manager or business owner cannot easily determine which costs increase and decrease with changes in sales, or what their overheads are for operating the business. It is essential to understand and identify each of the different costs and how they vary with

---

5   See Chapter 3: Planning, section 1: Framework, part 7: Can you compare the game of cricket to business?

activity. Often, a single business has various components or different activities that make up the total business. As an example, one of my client's company had three different businesses – secondhand vehicle sales, vehicle servicing and secondhand motor vehicle parts sales. This business owner's revenues were consolidated, and he did not know which activity was profitable and which was not. This leads to the next mistake…

3. *Not knowing which parts of the business are profitable*
So, did the business owner know if selling second-hand cars was profitable or whether it was worthwhile to continue to provide motor vehicle servicing? **No.**

Therefore, the *first step is to identify the different business activities*. Once this is done, *divide the revenue by activity* and then assign to the different business units – for example: secondhand car sales, spare parts sales and motor vehicle servicing.

The *next step is to categorise the costs by type*, variable or direct costs, indirect costs and overheads. Then *assign these costs into business units*. Overheads will be assigned to the consolidated business, with the P&L looking like Figure 14: Management P&L, XYZ Company on the next page.

XYZ Car Company

Management P&L

Sales Revenue as % of Total	Total		Car Sales 59%		Spare Parts 18%		Vehicle Servicing 24%	
	$('000)	%	$('000)	%	$('000)	%	$('000)	%
REVENUE	850		500		150		200	
Direct Costs	510	60%	300	60%	135	90%	75	38%
GROSS MARGIN	340	40%	200	40%	15	10%	125	63%
Indirect Costs	155	18%	85	17%	40	27%	30	15%
NET MARGIN	185	22%	115	23%	-25	-17%	95	48%
Overheads	150	18%						
NET PROFIT	35	4%						

Figure 14: Management P&L, XYZ Company

By reviewing the P&L, the business owner could see that spare parts was losing money. Vehicle servicing had a gross margin of 63% and was the most profitable area with a net margin of 48%. Furthermore, overheads were 18% of Revenue, which would seem high and may warrant further investigation. As spare parts was losing $25,000 per year, possible managerial actions could be to increase prices or cease selling spare parts, which would result in an additional $25,000 in profit.

These examples show what a good management or operations P&L should look like, and how managers and business owners can make informed decisions.

Remember, there are *three mistakes* in financial reporting:

1. Costs are incorrectly categorised
2. Reports do not reflect operational needs
3. Not knowing which parts of the business are profitable.

Does your current P&L allow you to understand the *cost drivers* and *profitability* of the business?

Is the P&L in a format that you can use to **improve your business's performance**?

Asian elephants were once found as far west as Syria

6.1.4 Is an annual budget really that important?

'The budget is not just a collection of numbers,
but an expression of our values and aspirations.'[6]

Jack Lew – US Secretary of the Treasury

In my experience, many small businesses do not have annual budgets. In fact, I have come across some multimillion-dollar businesses that do not have budgets, including several of my past clients.

What is a business budget?
A business budget is a financial plan and prediction of future revenue and expenditure. A budget is a goal for the business over the next 12 months.

Why are budgets important?
It's a goal – a plan – with three main purposes:

1. *A forecast* of income, expenditure and, by extension, profitability:
   Where are the costs incurred and where does the revenue come from to make a profit?
2. *A tool* for decision-making:
   It provides a financial framework for the decision-making process.
   It assists in courses of action that can be either planned or unplanned over the year.
3. *A means to monitor and measure* business performance:
   Where the actual business performance is measured against the forecast business performance.

---

6   Attributed to Jack Lew, 76th US Secretary of the Treasury, 2013-2017

In simple terms, all good businesses MUST have an annual budget. Otherwise, how will management or their staff know what is expected of them and the business?

How should budgets be compiled?

There are *two broad ways* of compiling a budget, either top-down or bottom-up:

1. Top-down is the less rigorous way of setting budgets and is more suitable for very small businesses. Often last year's results are reviewed, and a percentage added to revenue and costs.
2. Bottom-up is reviewing costs, customers, revenue, sales and other P&L items at a micro level, and determining what can be, and is likely to be achieved next year.

In my experience, based on having my own business and on what my clients tell me, bottom-up budgeting is the best method. It is important to invest the time in creating a comprehensive and realistic budget, as it will be easier to manage and ultimately more effective.

What are the suggested steps?

1. *Involve the right people*, including financial, sales and operational staff. Their involvement will help ensure their commitment to meeting the budget.
2. *Ask them for their estimates* on sales, production costs or specific projects based on first principles by referring to each line item and customer in the P&L.
3. *Rigorously question each assumption,* then get an agreement and a commitment from those team members

who are responsible for each part of the business. Ask questions such as:

- Which customers will increase their purchases next year?
- Where and how can we increase sales?
- Will we be able to increase prices?
- How can we reduce our fixed costs?
- What staff will get pay increases next year?

4. Only use last year's figures as a guide, and do not simply make broad estimates from these figures.
5. Complete the budget and share it with key staff.

In conclusion, the compiling of the annual budget is an opportunity to review and understand the business more thoroughly. A budget provides structure for the next 12 months, **imposes discipline** and **holds people accountable** for the business's performance.

What resources are required?

How many staff are required?

What customers are the most profitable?

Where can we reduce overheads and still increase sales?

Overall, budgets must be *realistic* and *achievable*, and should also be *aspirational* and not too easy to achieve. A budget should have **'stretch targets'**, to ensure the business grows. In all my years in business, I have never set a budget where revenue or sales were less than the previous year.

6.1.5 Why do airlines offer cheap seats?

*'I don't care what you cover the seats with
as long as you cover them with assholes.'*[7]
Eddie Rickenbacker – US aviator

Today, flying as a form of travel is widespread and growing, so we, the general public, are affected by airline pricing. Airline ticket prices are not set and can vary significantly, with some airlines offering flights that seem to be ridiculously cheap.

Why do they do this?
Modern airlines have very sophisticated analytical programs that use yield management or dynamic pricing to maximise the seating capacity of each aircraft, while obtaining the highest price for each seat. As Rickenbacker's quote implies, seats need to be filled. This is a concept relevant to many businesses, which is little understood. It is called **marginal pricing** and, if used carefully, can significantly increase a business's profits.

What is marginal pricing?
Marginal pricing occurs when a business sells a product or service at a price that covers the variable cost of producing it. The marginal cost is the variable cost of producing an additional unit or service. The concept of marginal pricing assumes that the fixed costs and over-heads are already covered by earlier sales[8].

---

7   Attributed to Eddie Rickenbacker, US World War I fighter ace and CEO of Eastern Airlines

8   See Chapter 6: Profits, section 1: Measures, part 3: What are the three major mistakes business owners make with financial reporting?

How does marginal pricing work in practice?

With airlines, the marginal costs of getting additional revenue are very low. Once an aircraft takes off, the empty seat is gone forever. It is a *perishable commodity* and cannot be warehoused or sold on another day. The marginal cost of additional passengers is virtually zero. This is why airlines can offer what appears to be drastically discounted fares. The same can be said for scheduled truck deliveries with spare capacity.

The road industry provides a good example of how this works in practice. For example (refer to Figure 15), the cost of operating a semi-trailer is $1,600 per day including variable costs – fuel, finance, tyres and maintenance, loading and unloading – as well as fixed costs and overheads such as insurance, registration, depot costs and the driver's salary. This is based on traveling 900km per day and a freight carrying capacity of 22 pallets.

The semi-trailer is loaded with 18 pallets (82% capacity) with initial revenue of $2,160 ($120 per pallet).

- Fixed costs and overheads: $450 per day
- Variable costs: $1,050 per day
- Marginal costs: $5.56 per pallet (loading and unloading a pallet).

With a *spare capacity of four pallets*, there is an opportunity for the vehicle to fill this capacity by using marginal pricing. The assumption is that no extra variable costs such as fuel and tyres are incurred, and the *only additional or marginal cost is the loading and unloading of the additional pallets*. According to the concept of marginal pricing, providing the marginal costs of $5.56 per pallet is included, any additional revenue above this will fall to the bottom line as profit.

This is demonstrated in the following table:

Marginal Pricing: Semi-trailer delivery

Capacity - 22 pallets	22		
Number of loaded pallets	18		
Utilisation	82%		

Daily Calculations		Daily Total	Cost per pallet
1. Fixed Costs		$ 450.00	$ 25.00
2. Variable Costs			
Fuel	$ 450.00		
R&M	$ 300.00		
Tyres	$ 100.00		
Finance	$ 200.00		
Total Variable Costs		$ 1,050.00	$ 58.33
3. Marginal Costs			
Loading & Unloading		$ 100.00	$ 5.56
4. Total Costs		$ 1,600.00	$ 88.89
5. Revenue			
18 pallets @ $120.00 per pallet		$ 2,160.00	
Spare capacity - 4 pallets (22-18)			
Net Profit per Day		$ 560.00	26%
If load 3 more pallets on truck @ $80.00 per pallet		$ 240.00	
6. New Revenue (21 pallets)		$ 2,400.00	
Capacity - 22 pallets			
Number of loaded pallets	21		
Utilisation	95%		
7. Additional Marginal Costs			
(3 pallets - loading & unloading)		$ 16.68	
Net Profit per Day		$ 783.32	33%
8. Increase in Profits		$ 223.32	
% Increase in Profits		40%	

Figure 15: Marginal Pricing of Semi-Trailer Delivery

This example clearly shows that the addition of three pallets loaded onto the vehicle, with revenue of $80.00 per pallet instead of $120.00 per pallet, increases the revenue from $2,160 to $2,400, with profits increasing from $559.92 to $783.24 per day, or **40%**.

Within manufacturing, the *marginal cost is the variable cost of producing an extra unit of output.* Let's use manufacturing 1,000 wheelbarrows as an example:

- Variable cost of manufacture is $20.00 per unit
- Fixed costs are $10.00 per unit
- Overheads are $5.00 per unit
- Total cost per unit for a single wheelbarrow is $35.00.

The total cost for 1,000 wheelbarrows is $35,000 (1,000 x $35.00). However, the cost of manufacturing an additional 500 wheelbarrows is $10,000, as $20.00 per wheelbarrow is the variable cost of production. The manufacturer could sell the additional 500 wheelbarrows at $40.00 each and make a profit of $20.00 per wheelbarrow.

Marginal cost pricing is a valuable tool for businesses, providing an opportunity to increase profits significantly if managed, particularly with unused capacity, such as in a manufacturing plant and in services such as transport.

However, there are dangers in marginal pricing. As a manager, *you must know and understand your costs* and this includes the cost of the sales staff.

Are there opportunities in your business to increase profits by marginal pricing?

What are the dangers if you decide to implement this strategy?

6.1.6 What are three warning signs that a business is on the verge of failing?

'Failure isn't fatal, but failure to change might be.'[9]
John Wooden – American basketball player and coach

Sadly, hundreds of businesses collapse each year in Australia often owing millions to creditors and employees.

---

9 Attributed to US basket ball coach "Wizard of Westwood" UCLA John Wooden

As a business owner or manager, what are the **warning signs**?

Please remember, we have to be honest with ourselves, have an open mind and put egos and denial aside[10].

In *Good to Great,* Jim Collins says, 'confront the brutal facts'.

Here are three warning signs:

1.　**Revenue is dropping**

As a manager or business owner, measuring revenue and recording it month by month over a significant period of at least two to three years, is critical in understanding and managing the business. Many businesses have seasonal fluctuations. For example, retailers' revenues peak before Christmas and chocolate manufacturers' peak before Easter. It is important to understand the nature of your business.

Understanding the fluctuation in sales over the year allows you to manage your cash flow.

There is an **extremely important principle** in business that is often misunderstood:

'Revenue is different from sales, as revenue is money collected'

A sale is not a 'true' sale until you collect the revenue. It is important to have a cash flow forecast combined with sales and revenue recording to understand the implications and relationships.

A sudden drop in revenue could result in a business not meeting their legal obligatory costs, such as superannuation and tax payments. This is a warning sign that the business is in trouble.

10　See Chapter 2: People, section 2: Management, part 5: 'Denial is not a river in Egypt'

I once saw a business claim to have increasing sales with a major retailer, only to find out that most of the sales were on a sale or return basis. This business went broke.

2. **Cash flow shortage**
    Many businesses can be profitable but fail due to running out of cash to pay their creditors. *Cash is the lifeblood* of any business. For example, sales and profit may be increasing but, due to not being able to collect the sales revenue in time, the business runs out of cash.

    Here is a **second important principle** that needs to be understood:

    There is a massive difference between profit and cash.

    It is therefore very important to forecast and track cash flow. By using a cash flow budget, the discipline of collecting from debtors monthly can more easily be implemented. Running out of cash is a good indication that a business is in trouble. Debtors who are slow payers and are a significant proportion of a business's sales can put the business at risk.

    Alternatively, *paying creditors later can significantly improve a business's cash flow* and provide funds for expansion.

    In our logistics business, we tracked our cash needs six months ahead and then tracked them against our actual performance. Wages were over 35% of our overall costs. In Australia, wages are normally paid weekly, while collecting from creditors takes between 30 and 45 days. A single decision to outsource our production labour with 30-day payments terms released cash into the business, negating the requirement to seek external finance to grow the business.

3. **Opaque accounts**

Sadly, many business owners do not understand their accounts[11]. Many rely on their external chartered accountant to provide them with their profit and loss figures, which are often not delivered in a timely manner. Accountants tend to report profit and loss in terms of tax compliance, and rarely do the accounts provide an operating perspective.

There is a **third important principle** for managing business accounts:

'Variable costs, fixed costs and overheads must be clearly identified in the profit and loss statement.'

I had a client whose accounts were prepared and forwarded by their external accountant up to three months after the end of the month. The business had no idea what was making a profit. They only knew that the business made a profit. Following some discussions – and correctly categorising costs into variable, fixed and overheads – we determined that there were three businesses or sub-businesses and that only one was making a profit.

We immediately engaged a bookkeeper, broke the business reporting into the three businesses and set up the accounts to reflect the operating environment.

---

11   See Chapter 6: Profits, section 1: Measures, part 3: What are the three major mistakes business owners make with financial reporting?

Within six weeks, the owner was receiving P&L information no more than three days after the end of the month. In nine months, the business had grown by 50%, as they could concentrate on the areas where the business was profitable. The owner now knew his gross margins, breakeven points and profits.

What are the lessons?

While the **three warning signs of business failure are financial,** there are two other non-financial reasons for business failure.

The *first reason* for business failure is *poor management and systems*[12].

They are generally symptoms of poor leadership. Management systems, financial, sales and operational systems that are robust, timely and accurate are essential for managing a business, both on a day to day basis and for the long term. They enhance management's capacity to understand what is occurring in the business.

The *second reason* why companies fail is related to *the people in the business*.

For example, allowing the egos[13] of those in leadership positions to undermine the evidence by believing, and getting others to believe, that everything positive is due to your talents and genius – and anything negative is the result of another party or the government. This approach of internalising the positives of the business and externalising the negatives is not facing the brutal facts. Hubris and exaggerated outward confidence will mask the true situation of the business and hard decisions are not made.

The questions you need to ask yourself are:

---

12 See Chapter 5: Productivity, section 3: Consistency, part 1: The importance of standard routines and procedures

13 See Chapter 2: People, section 2: Management, part 5: 'Denial is not a river in Egypt'

Do you *recognise the signs* of a potential business collapse?

Are your *actions* and *attitudes* part of the problem?

What should you do now to *prevent* the risk of your business collapsing?

6.1.7 Risk management

'The kinds of errors that cause plane crashes are invariably errors of teamwork and communication.'[14]

Malcolm Gladwell – Canadian author and journalist

Being in business is a risk, and it is a challenge for businesses to manage that risk. Risk varies from business to business, from industry to industry and from country to country. Every business will have inherent risks. A business that handles cash, for example, is more susceptible to theft than a quarrying business with stockpiles of raw materials.

What is business risk?

It is an event or situation that has a *negative effect* on your business. This can range from additional costs caused by the risk to situations that threaten the business itself. *Risks can never be completely eliminated. However, they can be managed and controlled.*

There are **two broad** types of risk:

- internal risks that are primarily related to what happens inside the business
- external risks where events and actions affect the business from the outside

---

14 Malcolm Gladwell, *Outlier; The Story of Success,* Hatchette Book Group, 2008

Example of Risk Matrix

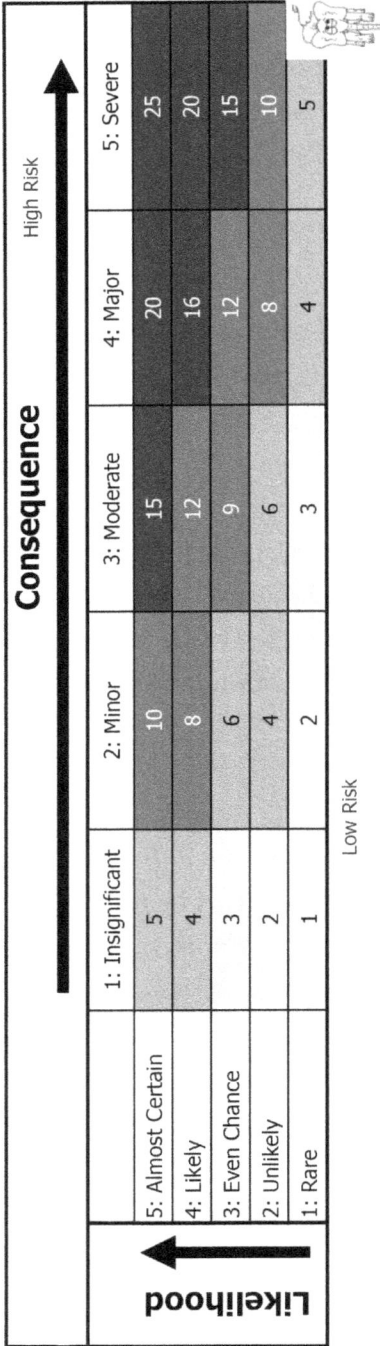

Likelihood	Consequence				
	1: Insignificant	2: Minor	3: Moderate	4: Major	5: Severe
5: Almost Certain	5	10	15	20	25
4: Likely	4	8	12	16	20
3: Even Chance	3	6	9	12	15
2: Unlikely	2	4	6	8	10
1: Rare	1	2	3	4	5

Low Risk

High Risk

Figure 16: Risk Management Matrix

As business owners and managers, it is our responsibility to manage business risk. For example, workplace safety is a managerial responsibility and a serious incident can have a substantial negative impact on the business[15].

How can business risks be identified?

- *The first step is identifying all the risks* that could potentially negatively affect the business. Discuss these initially with the management team, dividing them into internal and external risks. For example, in a mining company, external risks could include country or sovereign risk, weather risk, exchange rate risk and economic risk. Internal risks could include operational risk, safety, people, customers, events such as power outages and fire, and reputational risks.

- *The second step,* after identifying the risks, *is to assess each of the risks.* In my experience, the most effective method is to develop a risk matrix (see Figure 16) where severity or consequence is rated against the likelihood of the event occurring. Effective communication and consultation with the management team and other stakeholders will improve the quality of the risk assessment. For example, involve an expert in IT to help assess the risk of data breaches and system breakdowns.

- The third step, after assessing and ranking the risks, is to develop a risk management plan. There is an international standard (IEC/ISO 31010[16]) for risk management, which

---

15   See Chapter 6: Profits, section 3: Dangers, part 4: What is the cost of safety to your business?

16   ISO/IEC is a codified standard for risk management assessments by The International Organisation for Standardisation (ISO) and The International Electrotechnical Commission (IEC)

covers identification, analysis, evaluation, monitoring and
reviewing risk. This process is very detailed and involves
other disciplines such as finance, safety and human
resources.

The management of risks falls into four main areas:

1. **Avoidance** – eliminate the risk. A good example is
   decommissioning dangerous machinery.
2. **Reduce** – actions that mitigate the risk. In warehousing,
   where the risks of manual handling injuries are high, place
   limits on carton weights and have regular 'toolbox' safety
   meetings to reinforce the importance of using equipment
   safely and reporting heavy or awkward stock items.
3. **Share** – transfer, insure or outsource. Some obvious
   examples include insuring against events such as fire and
   accidents, and outsourcing transport services to a third
   party who have managerial expertise in this area.
4. **Retain** – accept the risk and have a plan to manage
   it. In transport, this could include improved selection
   of drivers, driver training and ensuring vehicles are
   maintained to the highest standard.

The risk management plan should have the identified risks listed
in a **risk register.** It should include the following:

1. Responses – actions to mitigate the risk
2. Contingency plan – plan if mitigation strategy fails
3. Risk rating – severity, likelihood and residual
4. Trigger – what is likely to trigger the risk occurring
5. Owner-manager or person responsible.

Although not all risks can be eliminated – and some risks are inherent in the industry or business – having a plan, monitoring and reviewing the risks regularly, and updating the plan when required is good practice. The collapse of McAleese Transport[17] is an example of how poor management of mitigating risks can have severe implications on a business and its employees. In conclusion, **the risk management plan should include a crisis management plan[18].**

What are the risks in your business?

Can you *categorise the risks* easily into consequence and likelihood?

Are they in your risk management plan?

---

17   See Chapter 6: Profits, section 3: Dangers, part 4: What is the cost of safety in your business?

18   See Chapter 6: Profits, section 3: Dangers, part 3: Can you manage a crisis?

6.2
Customers

6.2.1 Managing customer complaints

'Quality in a service or product is not what the supplier puts into it. It is what the customer gets out and is willing to pay for'[19]

Peter Drucker – author and business philosopher

As business owners or managers, some of the worst moments in your working experience can involve managing customer complaints.

The experience is often stressful, uncomfortable and unpleasant, isn't it?

Customer complaints have serious ramifications for your business and, if not managed well, can seriously damage the business. Customer complaints do, however, provide an opportunity to turn a negative into a positive and enable you to retain the business.

Remember: *it is estimated that less than 10% of customers complain about customer service,* they just go elsewhere, and we rarely know why. Don't dread customer complaints, but instead view them as an opportunity to create a long-term customer. **A complaint gives your business a second chance.**

There are **six steps** in managing a customer complaint:

---

19 Peter Drucker, *Management,* HarperCollins Publishers, Revised 2008

1. Let the customer vent their anger. *Remain calm, try and keep personalities out of the situation*, allow the customer to express their anger and listen attentively.

2. Make 'I' statements and apologise. *Build rapport and empathy* by using 'I' statements: 'I can understand… I would be angry'. Show that you are taking the side of the customer. The anger is addressed at the problem and not at you.

3. 'So, what you are saying is…' Try and understand what the problem is by using *effective listening* techniques – paraphrase what the customer is saying and ask clarifying questions so that you have a clear understanding of the issue.

4. 'This is what we can do….' Take *responsibility* for solving their problem and let them know what you can do. It is important to use positive language and offer solutions, options or a course of action. Make sure you gain agreement from them.

5. *End positively.* Thank the customer and explain what you intend to do, when and how.

6. Just do it. Just like the Nike advertisement, 'just do it' means providing updates, *following up* within the agreed time frame and communicating with them personally when that action has been completed.

This is an example from when I was managing a vehicle transport company. A transport manifest arrived by fax (yes, many years ago) at 4pm and, upon reading it, I learnt that there was a car arriving at our depot within the next two hours that was due in Brisbane that night. We were in regional New South Wales, 1,200km or 14 hours from Brisbane. The car then had to be loaded onto a truck bound north for Cairns a further 1,700km or 20 hours away. The car was needed by the customer in Cairns in two days' time for him to pick up from the airport and drive to his tropical beach holiday destination a further hour's drive north.

This was Mission Impossible.

It was a physical impossibility to have a car in Cairns nearly 3,000 km away in two days, even if it was driven there.

Flying a car to Cairns was not an option.

What happened?

I implemented the six-step approach.

With extreme dread, I called the customer and explained the situation three hours before he was due to board a direct flight from Melbourne to Cairns. Telling him that we could not help was not a sensible option.

His reaction **(Step 1)** was dismay, although not overt anger. How was he going to get to his holiday house?

I apologised **(Step 2)** and asked him again **(Step 3)** what his requirements for transport for his holiday were. He needed to have a car to travel to and around his holiday destination.

I then gave him several options, one being that we would provide a hire car at no cost for his entire holiday or until his own car eventually arrived **(Step 4)**.

He agreed, I thanked him for his understanding **(Step 5)** and said I would arrange this and get back to him.

A hire car was organised, using my personal credit card, to be available at the local Cairns airport lounge for his arrival **(Step 6)**. I then phoned him back just before he boarded the plane. He was very happy with the outcome. He continued to be a client for many years.

Even the most difficult of situations can be solved using common sense and the six-step approach to managing customer complaints…

Can you think of circumstances where this approach would have solved a customer service issue for you?

Customers normally want to know **how much you care**, not what **you know.**

6.2.2 Customer service

'Thank your customer for complaining and mean it. Most will never bother to complain. They'll just walk away.'[20]

Marilyn Suttle – American business author

I recently experienced not one but three examples of appalling customer service from a major Australian retailer, which has prompted me to reflect on what really is 'customer service'. I 'phoned two different stores and got the same result. The call was transferred through to the appropriate department until it rang out. I then phoned head office to seek assistance and was transferred to one of the stores again. After waiting for at least five minutes, a counter staff member picked up. He was most embarrassed and offered to get the department to call me. I refused, as I had had enough. My complaint via email to head office went unanswered.

Does that surprise you?

Recently, a business colleague told me the story of why, after 12 years, he had decided to sever the relationship with a major service provider and partner. Despite being a loyal and longstanding customer who always paid within terms, and his company being one of their largest customers, he had never met the CEO. When problems arose over service, the customer was accused of being inefficient and unreliable.

---

20 Attributed to Marilyn Suttle, an American work-life success coach

To cap it off, when the service provider finally met with the wronged customer to discuss the less than satisfactory service, she was told how busy he had been with other customers.

As a customer, do you care about a supplier's other customers and how busy they have been?

No.

You only care about your own requirements, as you are the one paying for their services. *You are not interested in their excuses.* They are not reasons. Such excuses make you feel as though you are not important enough to generate a relationship with. You certainly don't want to know that they were too busy taking care of another client.

Let's put it another way, no man (sorry for being sexist) would come home late for dinner and use the excuse to his spouse:

'Sorry I'm late for dinner, dear. I just caught up with my mistress for a quick drink.'

Like all relationships, whether family, social, personal or business, *the principles of common courtesy, respect, manners and decency apply.*

They are just as important in the professional or commercial world.

How are you going to **prevent** using similar types of excuses in your organisation?

What are the **steps** to make your customers feel that you are important to them?

6.2.3 Long term customer retention

'Customer satisfaction is worthless.
Customer loyalty is priceless.'[21]

Jeffrey Gitomer – internationally renowned expert on sales and customer loyalty

How many sales executives are given sales targets for new customers rather than nurturing and maintaining current customers?

Too often in business today, *the focus is on finding new clients – often at the expense of existing clients.* Generally, there are two types of salespeople with different personalities. They can be best described as either **hunters** or **farmers**. In the business sales process, they have different roles. A hunter's role is a sales role – find new clients. A farmer's focus is maintaining accounts and developing long-term relationships with existing customers – an account management role.

Characteristics of Sales People	
Hunter	**Farmer**
• Aggressive	• Even temperament
• Motivated by the challenge	• More co-operative
• Individuals	• Team approach
• Can be difficult to manage	• Much easier to control
• Lack of attention to detail	• Will complete paperwork
• Likes new relationships	• Nurtures existing relationships
• More short term	• Has long term view

Figure 17: Characteristics of Sales People

---

21 Jeffrey Gitomer, *Customer Service is Worthless,* Bard Press, 1998

Attracting new customers is a challenge and, although it can be rewarding, it involves planning and hard work – and it costs money. International consultants Bain & Company[22] found that the cost of attracting new customers was seven to eight times more expensive than retaining existing customers. They also found that an increase of 5% in retaining current customers could increase profits from 20% to 80%.

While acquiring new customers is important, *retaining current profitable customers is a far more cost-effective strategy*. Listening to current customers and actively seeking their feedback provides an opportunity to improve service, develop new services and provide a new source of referrals.

Remember: **over 65% of customers leave due to indifference.**

Do you have a system in place to *nurture* and *manage* current profitable customers?

I was providing advisory services to a business who were faced with two of their largest customers threatening to leave. There had been a history of poor service and strained relationships. Both client businesses were headed by difficult and often unreasonable personalities. Careful analysis of each business showed that one was not growing and was unprofitable to service, whereas the other was growing and profitable. To the credit of the business' general manager, and despite pressure from the owner, he took action. While he forced the unprofitable customer to leave, at the same time he developed a strong working relationship with the other customer, which resulted in the signing of a new contract with increased rates. The customer also recommended the business's services to another company. This is a good example of successfully managing an existing profitable customer.

---

22   https://www.bain.com

Are farmers more important than hunters as salespeople?
No.

It depends on the business's objectives. Both are needed for a business to grow. It is very important to maintain the *current profitable customers*, as it is cheaper for the business and offers other opportunities to improve and expand both services and products. The emphasis is on 'profitable' customers as, according to the Pareto Principle[23], not all customers are profitable. Making and maintaining sales need not be a difficult task. It requires an understanding of the business and must be aligned with the business's plan and goals.

Do you know who are your *most profitable customers*?

Why are they the most profitable?

Which customers are you *not making money from*?

6.2.4 Customer service - how much do you care?

'Your customer doesn't care how much you know until they know how much you care.'[24]

Damon Richards – American customer care expert

Actions speak louder than words. Customer service is about showing how much you care.

How often have you been annoyed or angry about being shown indifference by people in customer service roles?

There are 10 customer service actions you should implement in your business. In my experience, all people in custom service roles should use the words 'service' and 'action'. I will use the example of the 'car to Cairns' dilemma described earlier in this chapter.

---

23   See Chapter 6: Profits, section 1: Measures, part 2: Focus for success
24   Attributed to Damon Richards, US business consultant and customer expert

Here are the **10 customer service actions** and how they worked in that situation:

1. **Calling back when promised.** The customer was called back. After initially alerting him to the problem, he was called back within the 24-hour period, as promised.

2. **Explaining what caused the problem…in simple language.** I explained that it was our fault and we would have a solution for him not having his car on holidays.

3. **Letting customers know who and what numbers to call.** He was given my phone number and the Brisbane branch manager's phone number.

4. **Contacting customers promptly when a problem is solved.** As soon as the hire car in Cairns had been arranged, he was advised.

5. **Giving customers full access to speak to management.** I stated that if he was not happy with our solution, he could contact my general manager.

6. **Telling how long it will take to solve a problem.** He was assured that we should be able to solve the problem before he left for Cairns in three hours.

7. **Offering useful alternatives if a problem can't be solved.** As we could not physically get his car to Cairns on time, we offered him a hire car at no cost.

8. **Treating customers like people, not account numbers.** Self-explanatory.

9. **Advising customers on how to avoid a future problem.** It was suggested that he advise the depot next time he required his vehicle to be transported that it was 'IMPORTANT' and needed priority.

10. **Giving progress reports if a problem cannot be resolved.** While we solved his problem by offering him a hire car, he was contacted at every transport leg while the car was being transported to Cairns.

A seemingly impossible situation was solved using these 10 customer service actions. The customer was happy and continued to be a client for many years. As the quote implies, I could have told him it was impossible to get his car to Cairns in the time frame required – *'how much you know'*. Instead, customer service was demonstrated – *'how much you care'* – and he was happy.

These **10 actions** are so fundamental to good customer service that, in our logistics business, I had them framed and placed in every office.

Every 15 to 20 minutes, an elephant is poached

6.3
DANGERS

6.3.1 What are the dangers for profitability with family businesses?

'Forget "blood is thicker than water." That kind of mentality will send you straight into a financial hole you may never climb out of. Believing that your relatives feel they have as much at stake in the business as you, is a fallacy.'[25]

George Cloutier – American business author and philanthropist

Company profits can be likened to a bucket of water. As a manager or owner, you are responsible for keeping as much water (i.e. profits) in the bucket as possible and plugging the holes where profits are leaking out of the business. Plugging the **'profit leakage'** is more difficult to eradicate if the business has poor systems of management and governance.

As a former co-owner, with three other partners, of a business that employed over 100 people, I was clear about the potential issues with employing family members. Having worked for several family businesses beforehand, *you need very clear rules if you decide to employ family members.* I had witnessed the corrosive effect on profits of profit leakage when family members held significant positions in

---

25   George Cloutier, *Profits Aren't Everything, They're the Only Thing: No-Nonsense Rules from the Ultimate Contrarian and Small-Business Guru,* Hardcover, 2009

a business. From the managing director's brother who was totally incompetent, to a wife who held a significant position and had low people skills, they all led to lower profits.

Here are five circumstances where profits leak from family businesses:

1. *Family members have different rules to other employees.*
    I have seen situations where rules are bent or even ignored by family members. Having more than one standard can adversely impact profitability. However, this is rarely acknowledged, and particularly the impact this has on employee morale, as it affects motivation and productivity. For example, family members who are employed in the business may decide they have different timekeeping rules to other employees.

2. *Family members having a sense of entitlement.*
    We constantly hear stories of relatives employed in family businesses but not having the skills, training or temperament for their roles. It is essential to have clear roles and responsibilities, and everybody, including family members, must be held accountable for performance. Otherwise, profits leak through poor, suboptimal performance. Having worked in a business where the owner employed his son, I witnessed the corrosive effect that the son's poor work ethic and his sense of entitlement had on the business, garnering both poor morale and lack of respect for both the owner and the son.

3. *Maintaining the status quo.*
    As family members age, they often become resistant to change – stifling innovation and new ideas. Furthermore,

they can become complacent and often have other agendas. The one certainty about business is change, and anything that impedes change will lead to opportunities being missed and profits adversely affected. Business founders and leaders who stay too long in the business often stifle change where egos[26], rather than sound judgement, can be the basis of their decisions.

4. *High employee turnover, particularly high-performing staff.* There is no better indication of poor business health than top-performing staff leaving. In family businesses, when high-performing non-family members are passed over for promotion, they leave when they see the positions are reserved for relatives. There are hidden costs in employee turnover. Profits leak as time and money is spent on recruiting, training, and settling employees into their new positions, while non-performing relatives remain in their positions and continue to negatively affect morale. I left a senior managerial position many years ago when I was passed over twice for a promotion and the position was given to the brother of the managing director, who was incompetent and lazy, generating little respect from staff.

5. *Family tensions.*
Tensions arise in most families and, even if they do not have anything to do with the work environment, they have a habit of affecting the work situation. This can negatively affect morale and the efficient and effective operation of the business, and leak profits. For example,

---

26 See Chapter 5: Productivity, section 3: Consistency, part 3: Procrastination and egos cost business

I have witnessed situations where spouses who worked together were having domestic troubles. This severely impacted the running of the business.

What is the solution?

First, *recognise that it could be a problem*[27]. Put your ego aside, recognise the problems and deal with the issues in a rational and organised way.

Secondly, ensure that there are *good systems of management*[28] *and governance.* Clear rules on performance, accountability and behaviour are essential.

Finally, *make sure that you implement and enforce these rules,* and that management systems are followed. Furthermore, get outside advice and use a mentor or advisor. Their guidance and assistance can be useful tools to improve company performance.

Family businesses have significant advantages over large bureaucratic organisations, so don't allow the weaknesses to override the strengths. A family business can be more nimble, effective and profitable than a larger business.

Where do you think the *profit leaks* are?

In your family business, how will you *prevent* 'profit leakage'?

How can you *fix* these leakages?

---

27   See Chapter 4: Processes, section 1: Essentials, part 1: Problems
28   See Chapter 5: Productivity, section 3: History, part 1: The importance of standard routines and processes

6.3.2 Is there a thief or fraudster in your business?

'I take full responsibility for what happened at Enron. But saying that, I know in my mind that I did nothing criminal.'[29]

Kenneth Lay - disgraced criminal and former CEO of Enron

The following story was the result of a conversation with a friend. He is a partner in an IT business, and did not receive a promised payment. Ironically, their IT system had been hacked, diverting his payment to a fictitious bank account. Their customer did not have the checks and balances in their accounts payable department. However, **most fraud is internal.**

Is there a **fraudster** or **thief** in your business?

In the media headlines, we regularly hear about business fraud, from chief executives defrauding the company to cover gambling debts, to public servants giving contracts to family friends and associates, and to senior managers being appointed on false resumes.

However, fraud and theft in organisations are more widespread than the media portrays and are often hidden as it is embarrassing to the organisation and its management. Most theft and fraud occur *within an organisation*, not outside it. In Australia, theft in retail by employees is far higher than theft from shoplifting.

Every organisation needs to be vigilant wherever possible against theft and fraud and have the appropriate systems in place to prevent it occurring. I once worked for a company where it was rumoured that several of the senior managers were perpetuating fraud. The clue was that they were living beyond their means. An alert CFO decided to engage forensic accountants. The subsequent investigation found the

---

29   Kurt Eichenwald, "Crimes of Others Wrecked Enron, Ex-Chief Says" in *The New York Times*, 27 June 2004

fraud extended back over a decade and involved millions of dollars. The culprits were sacked, but it was never reported to shareholders.

For fraud or theft to occur there needs to be three conditions. This is often called the fraud triangle.

1. **Motivation** – this is often related to their personal financial situation and living beyond their means. For example, gambling debts. When I was in business, we had a customer who was defrauded for over $1 million by a 'trusted' employee who had gambling debts.
2. **Opportunity** – access to cash or goods and understanding of the company's systems. For example, truck drivers and dispatch staff in a warehouse colluding to steal stock.
3. **Rationalisation** – where employees often feel justified in their actions. For example, an employee who feels aggrieved by their salary or envious of the business or owner making a profit.

Most fraud or theft is a result of a *lack of segregation of duties*, *inadequate check and balance systems* and *inadequate supervision*.

In reducing the opportunity to steal or defraud, where do you start?

Like most things in an organisation, it starts at the top.

The **first step** is *the culture.*

1. Set the right ethical tone from the top of the organisation
2. Communicate no tolerance for unethical behaviour
3. Walk the talk and set the right example.

As a business owner or manager, you own the risk and it's your responsibility to identify the risk and manage it.

The second step is to ensure *internal accounting controls* are in place. Identify the areas of the business most at risk of fraud and focus your attention on improving controls in those areas, especially the ones relating to how money is moved around the business. For example, when paying suppliers and wages, separate out who can raise an invoice and who can pay it. Create a system where a second person is responsible for authorising payments that have been approved before the money leaves the organisation's bank account.

The final step is to *have a system* that will uncover fraud and theft. Two examples are:

1. Whistle-blower policy that protects the whistle-blower. For example, it may be a phone number an employee can call, such as the CFO. Most fraud is uncovered by employees.
2. Regularly and systematically analyse the data in high-risk areas, such as payroll and procurement, and investigate transactions that do not look right.

As well as being a management distraction when discovered, serious fraud and theft can destroy a company and jobs. In 2009, the CFO of listed Australian business Clive Peeters stole more than $20 million in less than two years. How this occurred in a listed company is hard to believe.

In over 30 years in business, I have witnessed too many acts of theft and fraud. In most cases, they continued until discovered and were the result of poor systems and supervisory management. Generally, theft and fraud start small and then, as the perpetrators become bolder and greedier, they become careless. Often, it's a small indiscretion that tips a manager off and it is the 'tip of the iceberg'.

In my work experience, two examples spring to mind. Personal items from motor vehicles were being stolen in transit. When the employees were caught, the police found an 'Aladdin's Cave' of stolen items[30]. In another example, a supplier was randomly checked, and the supplier was found to be owned by two managers who were directing non-existent services and collecting the money.

In conclusion, in your organisation, are you *vigilant about theft and fraud*?

Do you have the *necessary systems in place that discourage it*?

More importantly, do you set the *moral tone* and walk the talk?

Do you *set the standard* that theft and fraud at any level are unacceptable and will be dealt with accordingly?

Remember: a *fish goes rotten from the head first*.

6.3.3 Could you manage a crisis?

'It takes 20 years to build a reputation and five minutes to ruin it. If you think about that, you'll do things differently.'[31]
Warren Buffett – businessman, investor and philanthropist

In business, often *the hardest issue to manage is a crisis*. Crisis management should form part of your organisation's risk management plan. A properly developed and implemented crisis management plan can result in resolving the crisis, a continuation of business as usual, and preservation of your organisation's reputation and financial stability.

---

30   See Chapter 4: Processes, section 2: Methods, part 3: Can see but am blind?
31   Mashesh Dutt Sharma, *Motivating Thoughts of Warren Buffett*, Prabhat Books, 2008

So, what is the definition of a crisis?

A crisis has three common elements:

1. It is a **threat** to the organisation.
2. It has an element of **surprise**.
3. There is a **short** decision time.

One of the worst examples of managing a corporate crisis was the BP oil spill in 2010, where 11 rig workers were killed and millions of barrels of oil spilled into the Gulf of Mexico. The crisis went on for months, billions of dollars of damage was done to the environment, BP's share price plummeted, and the CEO, whose incompetence in managing the crisis contributed to the disaster for BP, lost his job[32].

How should a crisis management plan work?

By way of example, many years ago I was a manager of a large trucking company in an Australian rural city when a major incident occurred that met the *three common elements of a crisis*:

1. It had the element of surprise.
2. It was a threat to the business in terms of reputation and financially.
3. A decision had to be made quickly.

In the very early hours of the morning, I received a phone call from the maintenance manager to say one of our trucks had crashed into a house in the city. The truck, a fully laden semi-trailer, had driven into a residential area and, finding it was in a cul-de-sac, had reversed into a house, partially destroying the front bedroom. To add to the drama, inside the bedroom was a young, mentally disabled adult. When she

---

32   See Chapter 2: People, section 1: Leadership, part 4: Is leadership an art?

heard the truck backing into her room, she became hysterical. You can only imagine how stressed the family was.

In the initial telephone conversation with the maintenance manager, I did not recognise the driver's name, so I drove to the police station to try and identify him. When I arrived, I could not identify the driver, who was apparently drunk. Further confusing the situation, it then became clear that he had broken into the transport yard and stolen the truck. It would have been even worse if the truck thief had driven up the highway drunk, crashed into car and killed a family.

So, was the trucking company responsible?

Technically, *we were not responsible* as the driver was not an employee, had stolen the vehicle and was drunk.

Was denying responsibility and walking away from the incident a sensible action?

No. Unlike BP in the Gulf of Mexico's oil spill, we immediately implemented our crisis management plan. This included a *clear communication strategy*, in stark contrast to the BP situation.

We had to act quickly.

The family was immediately placed in a motel. Working with the police, we released a media statement to the local radio station, newspaper and TV station, explaining what had happened and what we were doing for the family. Repairs to the house were organised and completed. Within two weeks, the family moved back in.

The company's reputation was enhanced in the community. As we were already one of the largest employers in the city, we were now also seen as being the most socially responsible. The family affected formally thanked us, the business was not financially threatened, and business continued as usual[33].

---

33 *Post Note:* The driver gave the police several false names – however, he was eventually identified by his tattoos. He was charged, convicted and sentenced for vehicle theft, drunken driving and malicious damage.

So, does your organisation have a *crisis management plan*?

If not, I would recommend developing a crisis management plan and *testing it*, something that BP failed to do.

6.3.4 What is the cost of safety to your business?

*'The purpose is clear. It is safety with solvency.
The country is entitled to both.'*[34]

Dwight D, Eisenhower – former US president

Industrial safety, occupational health and safety (OHS), and now work health and safety (WHS) are becoming increasingly more prominent in the media, with government safety agencies regularly running high profile media campaigns that tug at your emotions.

Many business owners see safety as an overhead cost that should be avoided where possible.

Is this good business practice?

Can poor safety be financially detrimental to your business?

Many business owners would see it as a risk worth taking.

Is it?

In 2014, McAleese, a major Australian transport company, lost nearly $100 million of business primarily due to their poor safety record – highlighted by a fatal accident that caused the death of two people. A major multinational company would not allow them to tender on a major fuel contract because of their substandard safety record. The ramifications went further – $239 million was wiped off their listed value and 540 jobs were lost. The business eventually went into liquidation.

---

34   Public Papers of the Presidents of the United States: Dwight D. Eisenhower 1958

Poor safety is often a symptom of poor systems and management.
If safety is poor, it is likely that there are other major issues with the
business. By way of example, I managed a major interstate transport division for a public company where the managing director was
passionate about safety. The evidence was clear – vehicle servicing
schedules, management of driver hours, no speeding trucks, clean
trucks (which are a good sign of a well-managed transport business),
driver training and rigorous selection.

The evidence of success for the division I managed was emphatic –
low driver turnover, high truck utilisation, high profitability and no
fatal accidents in the six years I managed the business.

How was it done?
It was quite simple. A management system was implemented where
the 120 drivers' performance was reviewed weekly, they were involved
in managing their own performance, driver selection criteria was
rigorous and maintenance schedules were strictly adhered to. Supervisors and drivers were involved, and a culture of safety was supported
by senior management[35].

As a business owner or manager, next time you wish to cut corners
for safety keep in mind the consequences.

Remember to ask the question: *'is the business at risk?'*

---

35 See Chapter 5: Productivity, section 2: Change, part 3: Managerial discipline – are you
   chasing field mice or antelopes?

7
CONCLUSION

What can we learn from trying to eat an elephant, in relation to managing an organisation or owning a business?

How does this align with five dimensions (Ps) of business success: people, planning, processes, productivity and profits?

The answer?

When confronted with challenges, problems, tasks or opportunities, **'eat the elephant'** one bite at a time. That takes discipline!

A farming analogy demonstrates the alignment of the **Five Ps** and eating an elephant. My father purchased his farm from his father in the early 1960s. It consisted primarily of hills of undeveloped pasture with some plains which were suitable for cultivation. My grandfather only ran sheep for wool and a very small herd of cattle. The property of nearly 1,000 hectares was divided into five paddocks. This meant that it took all day to muster the sheep.

My father left school at 15. He had no post-secondary education, although he did attend technical college to learn wool classing. As a young man, he was relatively ambitious and inquisitive – a thinker who wanted to make a success of the farm, despite its relatively undeveloped state. He had a clear vision to develop the property and make it more productive in a sustainable way. It was like eating an elephant. Where do you start a large project to develop the farm with limited capital and resources? By having a clear vision and ambition, combined with realistic and attainable bite-sized goals.

People

With significant foresight, together with some of the more progressive farmers in the district, he recruited a tertiary-educated agricultural consultant to provide practical and scientific agricultural advice. This was 'getting the right people'. Due to market conditions and other risks, having wool as a single source of income was not a sensible long-term, sustainable strategy. With the assistance of the agricultural consultant's advice, the overall plan was to diversify the income base and increase the farm's productivity.

Planning

The first goal was to divide the property up into smaller paddocks to make managing the livestock more efficient. No more day-long musters like in my grandfather's time. This presented a problem as Plan A, erecting fences, was expensive and capital was limited. However, my father had noticed that dairy farms were using single wire electric fences to manage pasture use. Electric fences had never been really considered for use in the pastoral industry in Australia.

Although more traditional fences were preferred, electric fences with multiple electric wires (due to their cost effectiveness) became the Plan B. He was one of the first farmers in Australia to use electric fences in this way.

Process

The next problem was to increase the stock-carrying capacity of the smaller paddocks. Traditionally, sheep and cattle grazed on wire-grass, a hardy and not very nutritious native grass. The wire-grass seeds also lodged in the sheep's wool and reduced its quality and market price. Another challenge was to solve the problem of water for the stock, as the only reliable sources were a creek, which did not flow through the proposed new smaller paddocks, and a town water-supply dam on the edge of the property.

However, with careful planning, combined with professional advice and assistance, the farm's plan was achieved by a series of small, tangible and achievable goals. Loans were approved to finance the project. Dams were built in the gullies in each of the smaller paddocks, thus solving the water issue. The cheaper and very effective electric fences kept the stock in the smaller paddocks, and the stock ate out the poorly nutritious wire-grass. Once eaten out, the stock moved to the next paddock.

Productivity

So, what happened to the paddocks with no wire-grass?

Were they left bare and desolate?

No.

The next step was to increase the carrying capacity by introducing more nutritious grasses for the stock. Superphosphate, an agricultural fertiliser, was spread by aircraft to improve the soil and this was followed by aerial seeding of clovers and more nutritious grasses.

Each step was carefully planned and broken down into 'bite sized' goals that were measurable and achievable. They were achieved over several years and included the challenge of a severe drought. The plan was underpinned by discipline, hard work, focus and a clear vision.

Did this lead to an increase in productivity?

Yes.

Profits

Sheep and cattle numbers increased through using the new pastures and smaller paddocks, the farm diversified away from wool sheep to fat lambs (for meat), cattle were introduced and the areas suitable for cultivation were used for growing crops, mainly wheat. Within five years of commencing this project, my father won the local wheat quality competition. He later became one of the leading breeders of Limousin cattle in Australia, winning prizes at capital city shows.

...and it resulted in more profits.

What were the lessons?

- Success involves putting learning and experience to work
- Business is hard and the courage to fight and overcome is required
- There is power in having a clear vision
- Discipline, goal-oriented focus and planning are essential
- Small steps lead to achieving the large goal
- Measure and question everything

*'Someone's sitting in the shade today because
someone planted a tree a long time ago.'*[36]

Warren Buffett – business magnate, investor, and philanthropist.

The five Ps of a successful business:

people + planning + processes + productivity = more profits

Completing this book was like eating an elephant. At times, it looked as though I would never finish it and that it was too big a project. How did I do it? With the encouragement and support of others who revised, made suggestions and ensured I maintained discipline and, by taking 'small bites', met the goal. I did it! You can do it, too.

---

36   Andrew Kilpatrick, *Of Permanent Value: The Story of Warren Buffett*, Andy Kilpatrick
Publishing Empire, 2004

8
GLOSSARY

BFS – Boiling Frog Syndrome: a fable that describes a frog being placed in warm water which is slowly heated, and the frog is eventually boiled alive. It's a metaphor for explaining the consequences of ignoring the dangers of gradual change.

Discretionary Effort: the difference in the level of effort one is capable of bringing to an activity or a task, and the effort required only to get by or make do. In other words, 'going the extra mile'...

EBM – Elvis Business Model: a description of a business that is able to prosper and grow without the owner or CEO having to work in the business. Elvis Presley's business is worth many times more now than when he died over 40 years ago.

Gross Margin: sometimes called your gross profit but it is NOT profit. It is the net sales revenue minus the direct or variable costs (or COGS – cost of goods sold)

'I' Strain: an affliction of people with low emotional intelligence and large egos. 'I did this', 'I did that' and 'I am very important just listen to me'.

KBS© - Koala Bear Syndrome©: a description of employees who have koala type characteristics and appear to be a 'protected species'. They produce little, underperform, lack energy, are lazy, continually make the same mistakes, are incompetent and, more importantly, appear to be protected by their managers.

KISS Principle (keep it simple stupid): a description of how to explain something in easy to understand ways.

KPI – Key Performance Indicator: is a measure used to track performance of a business or activity. They can be either a lead indicator showing what performance is likely to be in the future, or a lag indicator showing past performance against specific measurable criteria.

KPQ – Key Performance Questions: are questions that assist in objectively developing activity measures (KPIs) to meet the business's goals.

Marginal Pricing: a little understood business concept and it occurs when a business sells a product or service at a price that covers the variable cost of producing it. Marginal pricing assumes that the fixed costs and overheads are already covered by earlier sales.

NDP – No D%ckhead Policy: a policy of not tolerating destructive personalities, egos and disruptive behaviour in a team or organisation.

P&L – Profit and Loss: the financial statement that summarises revenue, costs (variable/direct, fixed and overheads) over a specific period of time. Essential for managing any business.

PDSA Cycle – Plan-Do-Study-Act Cycle: system of continuous improvement with imbedded learning based on the 'Deming management method' of quality improvement.

RDS - Relevance Deprivation Syndrome (RDS): an affliction of retired politicians and business leaders who are distressed at losing their high profiles and power.

SWOT – Strengths Weaknesses Opportunities Threats: a process of identifying and organisation's internal strengths and weaknesses, and external opportunities and strengths.

W5H Check © – Why Where When What Who How: process improvement methodology used to improve productivity and by extension profits.

5 Whys: is a methodology used by the Toyota Motor Corporation to find the root cause of a problem, not the symptom. The method involves asking 'Why …?' five times in succession.

80/20 Rule: also known as the Pareto Principle where 80% of the effects come from 20% of the causes. For example, 80% of a business's profit will normally come from 20% of its customers.

9
BIBLIOGRAPHY

Gyles Brandreth, *Messing About with Quotes*, Oxford University Press, 2018

Warren Buffett, *Warren Buffett on Business: Principles from the Sage of Omaha*, Wiley & Sons, 2009

Bob Burg, *The Go-Giver: A Little Story about a Powerful Business Idea*, Portfolio, 2007

Dale Carnegie, *Who to Win Friends and Influence People*, HarperBusiness Classics, 1936

Lewis Carroll, *Alice's Adventures in Wonderland*, 1865

Jim Collins, *Good to Great: Why Some Companies Make the Leap and Others Don't*, Random House, 2001

Jim Collins, *Built to Last: Successful Habits of Visionary Companies*, HarperCollins Publishers, 2004

Stephen R Covey, *The Seven Habits of Highly Effective People*, Free Press, 1989

Will Cuppy, *How to Become Extinct*, Farrer & Rinehart, 1941

John Dewey, *How We Think*, Heath and Company, 1910

Peter F Drucker, *Management*, HarperCollins Publishers, Revised 2008

Peter Drucker, *The Essential Drucker*, HarperCollins, 2008

Peter Drucker, *The Practice of Management*, Harper & Row, 1954

Michael E Gerber, *The e-Myth Revisited – Why most small businesses don't work and what to do about it*, HarperCollins Publishers, 1995

Jeffrey Gitomer, *Customer Service is Worthless*, Bard Press, 1998

Malcolm Gladwell, *Outliers: The Story of Success*, Hatchette Book Group, 2008

Daniel Goleman, *Emotional Intelligence*, Bloomsbury Publishing, 1996

Charles Handy, *The Age of Unreason*, Random House UK, 1989

Verne Harnish, *Scaling Up: How a Few Companies Make It... and why the Rest Don't*, Gezelles, 2014

Heiner Karst, *Life Learnings of a Life Coach*, Major Street Publishing, 2012

Stephen Keague, *The Little Red Handbook of Public Speaking and Presenting*, Createspace Independent Publishers, 2012

Andrew Kilpatrick, *Of Permanent Value: The Story of Warren Buffett*, Andy Kilpatrick Publishing Empire, 2004

Kevin Kruse, *15 Secrets Successful People Know About Time Management*, The Kruse Group, 2018

Manning Marvel and Leith Mullings (Editors), *Let Nobody Turn Us Around: Voices on Resistance, Reform, and Renewal an African American Anthology*, Rowman & Littlefield Publishers, Maryland, 2009 (2nd Edition)

Andre Maurois, *The Art of Living*, translated from the French by James Whitall, English University Press, 1940

John J McCarthy, *Why Managers Fail…and what to do about it*, Paul Hamlyn, 1978

Mashesh Dutt Sharma, *Motivating Thoughts of Warren Buffett*, Prabhat Books, 2008

Simon Sinek, *Start with Why – How great leaders inspire everyone to take action*, Penguin Group, 2009

Richard S. Tedlow, *Denial – Why business leaders fail to look facts in the face – and what to do about it*, Penguin Group, 2011

Brian Tracy, *Eat That Frog!: 21 Great Ways to Stop Procrastinating and Get More Done in Less Time,*, Berrett- Koehler Publishers, 2017

Fred Trueman, *Fred Trueman's Book of Cricket*, Pelham Books, 1964

Sam Walton and John Huey, *Sam Walton – Made in America*,
  Random House, 1999

Andrew Webster, *Supercoach: The Life and Times of Jack Gibson*,
  Allen & Unwin, 2011

www.ingramcontent.com/pod-product-compliance
Lightning Source LLC
Chambersburg PA
CBHW031842200326
41597CB00012B/235